Wings Over the Sea

Wings over the Sea

The Story of Allan Moses

L.K. INGERSOLL

GOOSE LANE

Published with the assistance of the Canada Council and the New Brunswick Department of Tourism, Recreation and Heritage, 1991.
Photographs appear courtesy of the American Museum of Natural History (AMNH), Bowdoin College (BC), the Cleveland Museum of Natural History (CMNH) and the Grand Manan Museum and archives (GMM).

Cover photos: Allan Moses on Machias Seal Island, off Grand Manan, 1952 (NFB); L.K. Ingersoll and Allan Moses on Grand Manan, 1952 (NFB).
Map of Grand Manan Archipelago by Gillian Malins.
Book design by Julie Scriver.
Printed in Canada by Ronalds Printing.

Canadian Cataloguing in Publication Data

Ingersoll, L.K., 1914-
   Wings over the sea

   Includes bibliographical references
   ISBN 0-86492-101-2

1. Moses, Allan.   2. Conservationists — New Brunswick — Biography.
I. Title.
QH31.M67I63 1991   333.95'16'092   C91-097558-2

Goose Lane Editions
248 Brunswick Street
Fredericton, New Brunswick
Canada E3B 1G9

In grateful appreciation of the members of three generations of one special family, whose combined skills, knowledge and concern created what is now the Moses Memorial Collection of Natural History at Grand Manan Museum.

The blubird carries the sky on his back
— Thoreau

Contents

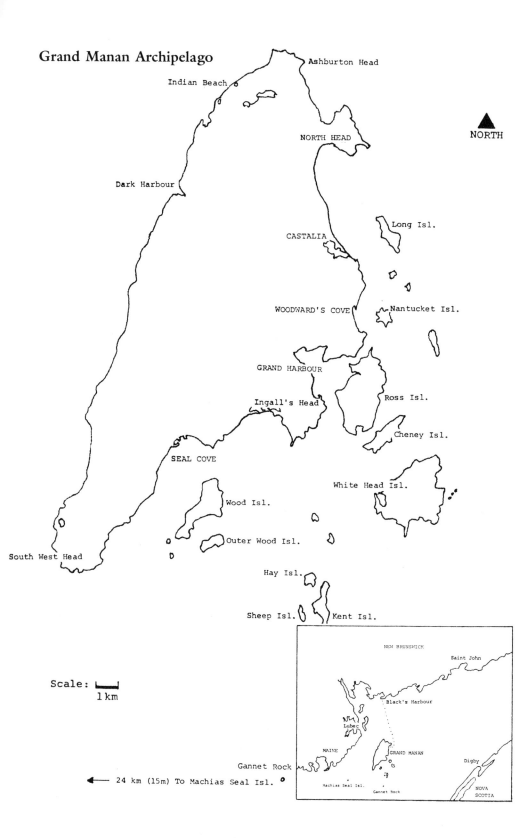

Grand Manan Archipelago

Ashburton Head

Indian Beach

NORTH HEAD

NORTH

Dark Harbour

Long Isl.

CASTALIA

WOODWARD'S COVE

Nantucket Isl.

GRAND HARBOUR

Ingall's Head

Ross Isl.

Cheney Isl.

SEAL COVE

White Head Isl.

Wood Isl.

South West Head

Outer Wood Isl.

Hay Isl.

Sheep Isl.   Kent Isl.

NEW BRUNSWICK

Saint John

Black's Harbour

Lubec

MAINE

GRAND MANAN

Digby

Gannet Rock

Machias Seal Isl.

Gannet Rock

NOVA SCOTIA

Scale: ⌐

1 km

◄ 24 km (15m) To Machias Seal Isl.

Foreword

GRAND MANAN IS a place apart. Not only is it an island of great natural beauty, its archipelago full of fascination, but its people have a sturdy independence reflecting their close contact with Nature, in all its beauty but also its rigours. Their pride in their island is shown in a variety of ways — not least, perhaps, in their own Centennial Museum. This was an Island venture in conception, development and erection, assisted by "mainland" funds that in 1967 were made available country-wide to help Canadians mark the centenary of their Dominion.

Centrally located on the Island's main highway, immediately opposite the High School at Grand Harbour, the Museum is now a centrepiece in the Grand Manan community. All visitors to the Island should visit the Museum; the majority do so, to the extent of many hundreds every summer. And it is the centre for year-round activities such as a summer nature school and regular meetings of the local Historical Society.

Within the pleasing, simple building, the centre of attraction is a magnificent collection of preserved birds, well exhibited in simple cases. Avid bird-watchers look with envy at perfectly mounted specimens of birds they may have always hoped to see while on the Island. The collection would be remarkable if encountered at a major mainland museum. How then did it come to be the treasured possession of this particular institution? This book happily provides the answer, since the collection was the creation of Allan Moses, with assists from two previous generations of his family.

It was, however, only one of the achievements of this remarkable Islander, albeit the only one now in public view. His name is still known on Grand Manan, still cropping up in leisurely talks if older people are present. But full appreciation of his quite outstanding activities is now restricted to the few and, quite naturally, the significance of his name is slowly fading as the years go by. The time was ripe, therefore, for a full record of his life and work to be prepared as a permanent memorial.

The contents of this volume show clearly how fortunate Allan Moses has been in his biographer. Keith Ingersoll has been a diligent and fruitful "recorder" of many aspects of Grand Manan life. All who have known both men, as I have been privileged to do, will rejoice in the linking of two notable Islanders. I count it a privilege to add these words to a volume that will rightly take its place in the growing number of biographies of outstanding Canadians.

Robert Leggett
Ottawa

Author's Preface

A REMARKABLE SERIES of events highlighted the career of Allan L. Moses. How they were made possible through his work as a naturalist, and brought rich benefits to people — and birds — on both sides of the Canada-United States border, will be told in the pages that follow.

Until now, only fragments of the story have been recounted and they have not always been accurate. The overall purpose of this work is to record, in a factual manner, the more notable experiences and achievements of a man whose entire life was devoted to nature and the preservation of the natural blessings which have been endowed upon this part of the world.

Through his initiatives and benefactions, and his challenges to others, his causes are still being pursued and with ever widening results. Like a number of New Brunswick achievers, however, his efforts have been more widely known outside the province.

Allan Moses was a conservationist, but he did not hold the idea that rare birds should never be killed. Today, some may question the many references in this book to "collecting" birds. W. Austin Squires, in his definitive book, *The Birds of New Brunswick*, explains that before the availability of powerful binoculars (and, one may add, high-speed cameras and films), "the professional ornithologist had to collect every unusual bird in order to satisfactorily identify it. At that time also," he points out, "all the major natural history museums were building up their collections of bird skins so that their series for each species would permit a critical study of all plumages and variations." Even now, collecting licenses are still issued to a few scientists, who must place their specimens in recognized collections. Citing as an example the eventual identification of a king rail found near Point Lepreau, New Brunswick, which was distinguished from a clapper rail only after close study of the skin, Dr. Squires adds this admonition: "When the collection of a single bird specimen can be so scientifically important sentimentality should not be permitted to interfere with it." He goes on to explain that in the light of the high natural mortality rate among most birds, the collecting of a few specimens is without statistical significance. Like other scientists of his time, Allan Moses collected bird specimens.

A similar leeway needs to be allowed the quotations from Allan's long journal-letters. I have condensed these letters somewhat, but I have not bowdlerized them. Allan Moses tells his story in his own words. What readers of today might find racist or culturally condescending must be seen in context, as expressions of his times and the prevailing Western Christian culture.

This story should have been underway, or at least in preparation, long before the subject's death. Nevertheless, during the last twenty years of Allan's life, I got to know him well and, in spite of the considerable difference in our ages, we became good friends. He told me about many of his fascinating and often hazardous adventures, and I wish there had been more time, but suddenly it was too late.

If the reader notices detailed information not acknowledged as to source, let me acknowledge here that it came from my own notes made during our conversations, or from my own observations made during the time when some of the great events were taking place.

In its present form, the story could not have been told at all had it not been for Allan's sister, Sarah, the family "secretary." The dispatches from Allan's journals that she edited and the excerpts she then published in local newspapers, as well as copies of her personal correspondence, have been invaluable.

Involvement with the Moses story has led to some very personal experiences. In 1963, in order to be more effective in the work of the Grand Manan Museum and Nature Centre then in the planning stages, I reported to the American Museum of

Natural History in New York for an internship in museology. From the very beginning, it was a highly interesting and stimulating introduction to what has to be done "behind the scenes" for a successful operation.

I was impatient, nevertheless, to see visible evidence of two important specimens in the collections from every continent on the globe. At the first opportunity I visited the Department of Ornithology, and was provided the particular catalogue data. Then I was given temporary loan of an albatross specimen, outstanding to science when it appeared in the northern hemisphere, and two specimens of the tiny African green broadbill, discovered indirectly because the big seabird had wandered so far from its South Atlantic home.

Going down the long corridors in the direction of the Photography Division, carefully guarding the treasures related to Allan's career, I thought of how much they meant to so many people, and to the conservation of other species. Though history and museums had been of concern to me for quite some time, it was only then that I realized the true value of the object to prove or supplement the written record.

Several years later, Dr. Charles Huntington, then director of the Bowdoin College Scientific Station at Kent Island, approached me about a problem in planning new studies in ornithology. Researchers at the Station were about to begin work with telemetry, as an aid in learning more about several species of birds, but the Canadian Government was not allowed to issue the necessary license to United States citizens. Since the units were miniature radio broadcasting mechanisms, the regulations were exactly the same as for regular, commercial stations, even though they were to be attached to feathered hosts.

As a result, I became the licensee for one of the then most extensive radio networks in existence. Of real importance for the reader is the information revealed by telemetry about the private lives of some of the Kent Island eiders.

Finally the memory of a warm individual whom I am proud to have had as a friend. In the more than five decades since I first made the acquaintance of Allan Moses, his stature has only grown in my opinion as I have recorded each facet of his career. *Wings Over the Sea* is an effort to share that appreciation with others and, at the same time, to serve as my tribute to a Canadian whose good works have been too little known in his own country.

I owe a debt of gratitude to those who devoted time and substance to the concept of a museum for Grand Manan: Reginald Carson, Donald C. Daggett, Jewett Green, Herbert Randall, Harvey Tatton, and Sumner H. Zwicker, in phase one; Merritt Brown, Marilyn Cary, Edith Cook, L. C. Cook, Ferdinand and Marion Eiseman, Earle S. Green, Otis and Marjorie Green, Gleneta Hettrick, Audrey A. Ingalls, Helen Ingalls, Joseph McDowell, Edith Miller, Donald K. Morse, Ernest Morse, Walter S. Ogilvie, Rowena Small, Eugene and Alice Somers, Charles Titus, Elmer N. Wilcox, and many others, in phase two, for the permanent program.

To be complete, the story of Kent Island must also include the resident keepers during the long-ago period when it was privately owned. These are, in sequence, Doddy Goodwin, Bartel Anderson, Newton Bryant, William Anderson, Terrance Robichaud, and Wilhiem Olsen.

I am grateful to a number of agencies and individuals for information, illustrations and general assistance. Included are the American Musem of Natural History, New York; the American Ornithologists' Union, publishers of *The Auk*; the Cleveland Museum of Natural Science; Grand Manan Museum and Archives; the National Geographic Society, Washington, D.C.; the Department of Natural Science, New Brunswick Museum; and *The Saint Croix Courier*, St. Stephen, N.B. Fitzhenry & Whiteside, Don Mills, Ontario, deserve special mention for permission to use Henry David Thoreau's one line poem from their *Book of Quotations*.

Particular thanks go to Dr. Charles Huntington, Emeritus professor of biology at Bowdoin College, and a long time director of the Kent Island Scientific Station. His successor, Dr. Nathanial Wheelwright, has also been very helpful. Dr. Robert M. Cunningham, the noted meteorologist of Lincoln, Massachussets and Grand Manan, has been especially kind. He has had the longest continuous association with Bowdoin's Kent Island, dating from 1937, and his assistance with that part of the story has been especially important.

Joan Wilson of Fredericton made the final typescripts, gratis. Her husband, Raymond Wilson, Jr., is a grand-nephew of Allan Moses, and through the couple I obtained access to their own family records, as well as information from an aunt, Helen Smith Frye of St. George, Allan's niece.

Dr. George MacBeath, a leading authority in history, and Peter Pearce, a wildlife biologist, both of Fredericton, read the manuscript and offered suggestions for improvement. The latter is also President of the New Brunswick Federation of Naturalists, and his liaison work led directly to the publication project.

Services both vital and various were contributed by Kathy Breau, Alma Cronk, Dr. W. Earl Godfrey, Gale S. McLaughlin, Winfred Moses, Norma J. Neves, Myhron and Eunice Tate, and Marie Thomas. Then, too, there is a long list of friends who generously supported the involvement by Grand Manan Museum.

In fond memory, I give grateful credit to Ruby Astor for her constant encouragement. I especially appreciated her patience and understanding, as she listened to long hours of manual typing. The part she played was, in many ways, one of the most important of all.

L.K. Ingersoll
Fredericton, N.B.

New Brunswick Travel Bureau

Allan Moses at the family museum on Grand Manan, 1946.

ONE

The Eiders' Circle

EARLY IN THIS CENTURY, an albatross wandering too far from its home in the South Atlantic indirectly caused a miracle on Grand Manan, an island in the Bay of Fundy between Maine and New Brunswick. "The Rime of the Ancient Mariner" had taught generations the legend that an albatross is a good omen, and that to harm one brings supernatural punishment. But, in this true story, a subantarctic albatross became a bargaining chip in North America's conservation history. Paradoxically, its death brought good fortune to another family of birds (and to bird lovers) when its life, and that of a rare central African flycatcher, was sacrificed for science. The human agent in this exchange was Allan Leopold Moses, a Grand Manan naturalist. A long-headed bargainer, Allan Moses originated a plan that since 1930 has provided a protected summer home for the common eiders of the Bay of Fundy.

Averaging two feet in length and up to three pounds in weight, the eider dwarfs most of its nesting neighbours. Its head has a long sloping profile, and the male in breeding plumage is the only duck on the northeast coast of North America with a completely white back above a black belly. The female, in contrast, is a deep brown colour, with the plumage noticeably barred in a deeper shade. Ornithologists may distinguish between two populations or races of eiders: "American eiders" (*Somateria mollissima dresseri*) and "northern eiders" (*Somateria mollissima borealis*). "American eiders" winter along the New England coast and southward but come north to nest at sites in and around the Bay of Fundy and the Gulf of Maine, while "northern eiders" breed along the upper reaches of the Gulf of St. Lawrence and the Labrador coast and winter in the Bay of

Common eiders, back from oblivion. Males in foreground. (BC)

Fundy. The two populations together are designated "common eiders" (*Somateria mollissima*).

The eiders to whom the dead albatross brought good fortune had nested from time immemorial on the Three Islands group, southeast of Grand Manan. Many believe that these islands, of which Kent Island is the largest, served as the main eider hatchery for all of the great Bay and beyond. By the time the sanctuary was established, however, the Three Islands flocks had nearly been destroyed. Smaller colonies along the coastline of Nova Scotia, New Brunswick and Maine had suffered a similar fate. The causes were fourfold: the commercial value of eiderdown; the delectable flavour of eider flesh and eggs; the challenge to hunters of a bird in flight; and, worst of all, wanton destruction coupled with ignorance of, or disregard for, the consequences. When Allan Moses first saw the need to make the Three Islands into a sanctuary, brooding females were even being shot on their nests.

The intention of the biblical mandate to humanity, "be fruitful and multiply and replenish the earth, and subdue it; and have dominion over the fish of the sea, and over the birds of the air, and over every living thing that moveth upon the face of the earth," is surely not to sanctify arrogance and tyranny. Domineering individuals, unwilling to recognize the difference between "dominion" and "domination," have continuously misinterpreted these words of wisdom, with the result that by the early part of our century many birds and mammals had already been driven to extinction. Humans are among the few predators who will kill more than they need for food, and humans alone place a commercial value on their prey. Even when killing for money is necessary for survival, humans were (and remain) willing to kill beyond their requirements, motivated solely by the challenge of a moving target.

The names of the lost species are familiar. The great auk, a flightless sea bird that once numbered in the thousands along the Atlantic coast, had disappeared by 1844. The passenger pigeon, migrating in flocks that "darkened the sun," followed later in that century. The Labrador duck, said to have been common once in the Bay of Fundy, became extinct in the late nineteenth century before much was known of its life history. Walrus were once abundant in the Bay of Fundy and along Maritime coastlines, but now they live only in Arctic waters. Woodland caribou once roamed the Maritime region, but by the beginning of this century they too had vanished. Scores of other species have gone from the face of the earth or survived by retreating to more remote areas, and many others are endangered.

Early in this century, the conservation movement began to try to care for natural resources so that they might continue to exist in a changing world. Thanks to the introduction of protective legislation and international treaties such as the Migratory Birds Convention Act, species such as the whooping crane and the peregrine falcon are recovering their niches in the world. And thanks to Allan Moses, the common eiders of the Bay of Fundy have made a dramatic comeback.

No doubt humanity will always selectively use the "lower animals" — those lower in the food chain — but respect for our natural blessings is growing, based on a recognition of the interdependence of all living things. The waters surrounding the Three Island group are a microcosm of this seamless web of mutual support. This has always been a place of plenty in the natural food chain — an ideal location for a sanctuary. The islands and surrounding ledges and shoals form natural barriers in the flow of the strong Fundy tidal currents. The narrow straits funnel the sea water and hasten its movement. Even the force of ocean waves, miles away, tends to keep Fundy currents in action. Food and other nutrients are churned to the surface by all these competing forces, providing the setting for a marine system that includes all the plants and animals needed in an interdependent chain.

During the Bay of Fundy summer, late June to late September, the breeding season of sea birds conveniently coincides with a high production of plant and animal life, boiling up to the surface waters from this garden of the sea. An abundance of plankton means food for tiny shrimp and other species that attract herring and other small fish. The chain grows and expands to include cod, hake and pollock, then tuna and sharks and the sea mammals — seals, porpoises and whales. Intertidal plants and animals play their part, while sea birds feed on the surface of the water and human hunters and fishers select from the bounty on and under the surface for their food-baskets.

Passamaquoddy Indians from Maine were summer transients in the Grand Manan area for thousands of years. They would arrive at what is now known as Indian Beach on the western shore of Grand Manan, only a seven-mile canoe trip from the Maine shore. There they would camp and hunt porpoise. From Indian Beach, by easy stages, they could reach Ross and Cheney Islands off the eastern shore, where they would feast on shellfish. Three more miles of paddling took the Passamaquoddies to Kent Island, where they enjoyed the bountiful seafood, and harvested sweetgrass to weave into baskets once they returned home.

In 1869, Dr. Spencer F. Baird, Secretary of the Smithsonian Institution and founder of the U.S. National Museum, proved that this had been a prehistoric travel route when he uncovered middens and shell heaps in both locations, and Indians were still using the route as recently as 1930. That spring, a party of Grand Manan men and boys set out to capture a heifer that had eluded the fall roundup of the cattle that had pastured on Kent Island over the summer. After wintering on the island, the heifer was as wild and quick as a deer, and they had to shoot her. Then the party called on a small band of Indians from Pleasant Point, Maine, camped nearby. They were preparing their main meal of the day, turning a young seal on a spit over hot coals, and they invited the heifer-hunters to join them. In spite of its tantalizing aroma, the shape and appearance of the roasting seal did not appeal to the visitors, so they graciously declined the invitation and bade the Passamaquoddies farewell. After 1930, the yearly visits of the Indians ceased.

Common eiders and their eggs formed a part of the native people's spring and early summer diet, but they did not waste or over-exploit nature's resources. They took just enough to supply their needs, as part of a discipline designed to perpetuate the balance of nature. This level of predation could continue while the world lasts. But the arrival of Europeans brought an end to that era. These newcomers, like the Passamaquoddies, had to have food, clothing and shelter, but over a period of some three hundred years their settlements grew and they added guns, sailing ships, and finally automatic rifles and motor boats to their store of destructive weapons. Centuries passed before they began to recognize the results of their undisciplined plundering and the wisdom of the native ways.

By 1929, when Allan Moses took the situation in hand, "several" common eiders were said to nest in the vicinity instead of the huge colonies of the past. Six years earlier, the naturalist Charles W. Townsend reported seeing only three or four individual eiders around the offshore islands during July and August; he considered them "nearly gone" even then. Because they suffered from gunning, the stealing of eggs, and the taking of down, the eiders were very severely threatened, but they were not the only birds using the islands. Guillemots, a large colony of Leach's storm-petrels, and a great many herring gulls, as well as a smaller colony of great black-backed gulls, summered there.

Wading birds of several types fed along the shores, and about fifty varieties of song birds could be seen, especially during the spring and fall migrations. In 1929, Kent Island had the largest colony of herring gulls on the Atlantic coast. The island was nearly two miles long but hardly one-half mile across its widest part, and its northern end supported a thick stand of spruce. A gigantic, noisy herring gull hatchery occupied the southern end of the island; the nests were so close together a person could hardly walk between them. Only three miles away, razorbills nested on the Murre Ledges, and a few miles south, at Machias Seal Island, Arctic and common terns and Atlantic puffins raised their young. Allan Moses once wrote to a friend at Harvard that, with all his experience, he had ever seen any place like the Three Islands area for the variety and number of interesting birds. The deal he made with Sterling Rockefeller to persuade him to buy Kent Island and turn it into a bird sanctuary marked the beginning of a dramatic turnaround for the eider population.

In 1935, during Depression times, the Rockefellers deeded Kent Island to Bowdoin College in Maine. In the half-century since, it has served as a highly successful outdoor laboratory, of which the bird sanctuary is an integral part. Naturalists and scholars observe eiders and all other forms of pulsing life in their natural habitat, study them, and protect them. The published results of their research continue to enhance human respect and appreciation for some of the "lesser" creatures of the earth.

TWO
Allan Moses and his Family

WHEN ALLAN MOSES was born, half a century had passed since his paternal grandparents had migrated from England. Yet the British ties were still strong and, like colonists throughout the Empire, the Moses family felt a sense of pride in ably meeting the challenges of living in a new land. But, as well as a desire for material things, the Moses family also maintained its traditional close relationship with the natural world and an eager curiosity about all of its secrets. Their new home on Grand Manan Island, out at the mouth of the Bay of Fundy, seemed an ideal place to satisfy both objectives.

In England, the family seat had been at Chelmsford in Essex. For generations they had been "grassers," owning and leasing extensive farm lands on which they raised sheep and cattle for the London market. Joseph, the first of the line with whom this account is concerned, married Mary Henson in 1804. Family records in the Grand Manan Museum Archives state that she was a direct descendant of an advisor to William the Conqueror. The consequent royal favours benefitted the succeeding generations in small yet important ways that, combined with industry and thrift, kept the Moses family in fairly comfortable circumstances.

They could afford to indulge in some of the fashionable hobbies of the period. When Joseph's son Henry returned from medical school in Germany, he brought home something more than the healing arts. He had been taught the skills of collecting and mounting birds for study and decorative arrangements, and he taught these skills to relatives back home. One of his brothers took up taxidermy with great interest; he was John Thomas Chiseldon Moses, and with him our story really begins.

John Thomas Moses was twenty-one when he followed his Uncle Thomas to America. Captain Thomas Moses was a British Army veteran, wounded in the Crimean War and given a small pension and a grant of land near Stanley, New Brunswick. With his wife and eight children, he sailed from Liverpool on August 31, 1831, aboard the William Pitt, landing three months later in Saint John. Before long, however, he gave up his grant of land and became the first customs officer on Indian Island in Passamaquoddy Bay.

Young John Thomas joined his cousins on Indian Island, and soon he married one of them, Miriam Anna Moses. John and Miriam were living in Bangor, Maine, when John Russell, the ninth of their ten children, was born in 1853. Several of their children eventually made their permanent home in New England, but in 1872, John Thomas and Miriam moved with some of their family to North Head, Grand Manan. While still in Maine, father and sons had been involved in the fisheries in Passamaquoddy Bay, and now they saw that the outer Fundy island was also a promising location for the study of nature. In 1876, the *Saint Croix Courier* published a book by J.G. Lorimer called *History of the Islands and Islets of the Bay of Fundy*. It contains what may be the first locally published list of Grand Manan birds, about which Lorimer notes, "The above list of land and sea-birds has been kindly handed to the author by our Grand Manan ornithologist, Capt. John T.C. Moses, a native of England, but long a resident of Charlotte County, New Brunswick, retaining ever an enthusiastic love of fatherland and the old flag. He makes birds his specialty and his pastime."

Miriam Anna died in 1884, the year the island was first linked to the mainland by regular year-round ferry service. John Thomas died a year later, but he had long since passed on his nature lore and taxidermy skills to his son John Russell. John Russell Moses, Allan's father, earned his first dollar catching harbour pollock on pin hooks in Passamaquoddy Bay when he was a very young lad. Though most of the local residents considered harbour pollock worthless, John Russell cured his catch well and found a ready market just across the bay in Maine.

That was the modest beginning of a long and highly successful career, first as a fisherman and eventually as an exporter of fish products. Allan Moses later said of his father that he had a good deal of "the Midas touch" — every business venture turned into money — and that he himself wished he had "inherited just a fraction of that talent."

For many years, John Russell was the major fish buyer in the northern part of Grand Manan, and he processed the fish at his large rambling plant at North Head. The catches included cod and pollock, but hake was the most plentiful species. The fish were salted and dried for export to Europe, the southern United States and the West Indies. The astute John Russell recovered hake sounds (air bladders), a usually worthless by-product, when the fish were dressed. He then dried them and sold them in the United States. Before the adoption of Prohibition in that country in 1919, dried hake sounds sold for as much as $1.25 a pound. They were used to make isinglass, an early form of plastic, which in turn was used in the brewing industry to settle, or clarify, beer. In an average year, the Moses plant produced up to ten thousand pounds of dried hake sounds and took almost a clear profit on that single item. On December 12, 1929, the Charlotte County weekly newspaper, the *Saint Croix Courier*, carried a surprisingly frank feature story about John Russell that called him "that captain of industry" and "King of finance" in the island community.

In 1877, five years after the family had settled at Grand Manan, John Russell Moses married Lydia D. Lewis of Centreville, Carleton County. Their daughter, Sarah Elizabeth, was born the same year. Allan Leopold arrived in 1881, followed by Bedford Roy three years later. The three children grew up in a home where much of the abundant love and warmth came from mother Lydia. In her quiet, efficient way she managed the household and never seemed upset when her husband frequently brought strangers home unannounced for a meal. Some of the steady flow of visitors were business associates, but most were professional naturalists or keen amateur bird watchers.

While he may often have been preoccupied by business and

birds, John Russell loved his family, too. His gruff exterior at times hid the fact that he had a kind and gentle nature. Though he treated his children fairly, he rarely overindulged them. He made sure they learned that everything in life had a price, and that rewards came only through honest effort. Whether there were guests at dinner or not, the talk around the table was almost always about the wonders of the natural world. This was especially true each spring and fall, since that was the time to discover new and different birds. The great migrations made bird watchers of the entire family. While the children were still young, their father began to collect and mount selected species of birds, along with sea shells and interesting sea mammals. These specimens ended up in their own building near the home, as the beginning of what was to be the Moses Museum. Allan's grandfather, John Thomas Moses, had prepared a number of specimens, the most notable of which was a cluster of a dozen beautiful birds perched on a cured, natural bush. Sarah, Allan and Bedford were surrounded by nature and came to love it all.

Allan's entry into the life of a fisherman, like that of many another island boy, began as a kind of recreation. On Saturdays and during summer holidays, he and Bedford learned how to row and scull a dory. First they played on calm days in the sheltered waters of Flagg's Cove, but later they found more of a thrill on windy days in riding the crests of waves rushing toward the shore. The challenge was to estimate the right time to turn back towards the sea, without rolling over into the churning water. An upset might be dangerous, but having one's dory actually driven up the beach was humiliating, hinting as it did of a certain lack of skill.

Rigging a mast and a makeshift sail on the dory transformed the humble little boat. Allan, Bedford and their friends could imagine they were aboard a real sloop — when conditions were just right — but they soon learned that the flat-bottomed dory was not the best kind of sailing vessel. When two of their friends appeared out in the Cove one day with a sail-rigged dinghy, they watched with envy. A keel made all the difference in the world between their dories and a real sailboat. Soon, Allan and Bedford owned their own dinghy, but only after they had saved up the money for a down payment from chores and odd jobs at the fish plant. John Russell supplied the rest of the money, not so much as a gift, he explained to them, but as an investment in a partnership. Soon, most of the boys in the little fleet were brave enough to sail outside the Cove, and they were all learning to fish. Their first catches consisted of sculpins and other "trash fish" that lived inside the Cove; then they started to land harbour pollock, sometimes mackerel and occasionally a flounder. More often than not, their fishing gear was a primitive copy of the real thing — cast-off codlines, net leads for sinkers and, when they were lucky, brand new medium-sized Mustad hooks bought for a penny or two at Gaskill's General Store.

Perhaps if life at home and around the fish plant had not been so interesting, Allan might have studied more diligently and had more success in school. As it was, school frankly bored him. The curriculum was limited to the "three Rs," and the lessons were usually taught by itinerant teachers who were often dull, however well meaning they may have been. Any reference to the world of nature that Allan had made his own was shallow and incidental, limited, as Allan recalled, to "getting a star for bringing in five spring flowers." He admitted that while he sat in the stuffy classrooms he dreamed of the real world.

Here was a lad who, before he was ten years old, knew that the herring gull was really *Larus argentatus*, whereas the farmer's gull, the great black-backed gull, was known as *Larus marinus*. At least, these were the names used by himself and his family and the interesting people who called at the family museum. And there were other things beyond the ken of the classroom. Down at the fish plant he had watched in awe as a fish splitter drew a fair-sized lobster, still alive and well, from the belly of a large cod. And did the teacher know that the lowly hake was equipped with an inflatable air bladder to help it get about its ocean home? There was so much to learn, but he couldn't do it confined to a desk for most of every day. Considering these circumstances, it is not surprising that Allan dropped out of school. The family urged him to continue. His father was even willing to send him to university, but Allan saw little point in going, since wildlife biology was still not in the curriculum.

Allan's first trip to the offshore fishing grounds with older friends opened up a whole new vista of the natural world. He tried to keep up with his elders as they hauled lively fish in over the side of the boat, but his attention was more on the sea birds that gathered around. The gulls and terns he knew, but there were others that were complete strangers. That experience, like so many others in the years to come, furnished topics for meal-time discussions in the Moses household. Everyone took part, with John Russell presiding. After supper, the books were brought out — the few books on bird and animal life then available. For the bird books to be useful, however, one had to remember fine details of a bird in flight, sometimes in view for only a minute or so. The ducks were fairly easy to recognize, but the little petrels, auks, murres, shearwaters and many others would take more time.

Allan saw getting out with the fishermen as another way to explore, to learn and to earn a living at the same time. In fact, after he discovered his flair for the sea, Allan wanted to spend the rest of his life as a commercial fisherman. But, promising as it was for earning and learning, full-time fishing had to be delayed for a few years yet. If Allan would not go to school, John Russell expected him to take his place in the expanding fish business, and Allan's work from early spring to late fall was centred around the Moses fish plant. He learned how to bait trawls, how to dress the fish brought in each day, how to salt them and put them out to cure in the wind and sun. He quickly caught on to all the tricks of the trade, and he soon became as deft as his elders with the hooks and knives. Hanging out hake sounds to cure on fences near the plant or on the drying flakes was not exactly an inspiring job, but it had to be done, because the little bladders were worth more than the fish. Handling cod livers was another unappealing task, but they had to be packed in oaken hogsheads to age. In due time, John Russell would sell the cod liver oil to a mainland company to be refined and sold in drug stores. Hake sounds made better beer and cod livers made a popular medicine; Allan neither cared for the one nor needed the other.

There was lots of work connected with the fish plant, Allan could handle it well, and for the most part he enjoyed it. But the finer points of buying and selling fish simply did not interest him, and eventually he joined the fishing fleet. Early each spring, he and his friends set hake trawls, then later they hand-lined for cod, pollock and haddock and, once in a while, they experienced the thrill of hauling in a prize halibut. As time passed, Allan became

Allan as a young man, c. 1910.

(R. & J. Wilson and Helen Smith Frye)

not only a capable fisherman, but an experienced boatman as well. He learned to handle a vessel under sail (gasoline motors for marine use were not available until he was over twenty-five years old), a skill that would stand him in good stead in the vocation he finally chose to follow.

Allan's true career did not lie in fishing either, and he came to regret his educational limitations. Family-tutored and self-taught in the natural sciences, with an inborn talent in that direction, he had a profound knowledge of the other creatures of the earth, especially birdlife. Throughout his career, however, especially when he had become a recognized authority in the still-new discipline of ornithology, he found his advancement and his reputation continually hampered by an inability to communicate effectively. Never at a loss for words or for knowledge of his field, he nevertheless found writing a formidable task. In small gatherings, he shone, holding informal study groups spellbound, but he found public speaking an impossible burden.

The education of Allan's older sister, Sarah, took a different

Sarah E. (Moses) Smith, c. 1900.

(Helen Smith Frye)

path, although finally brother and sister worked as a team. When Sarah finished public school, she, like Allan, could very well have gone to college. She certainly had the ability, and her father had the means to pay her way. But going to college was not yet the fashionable thing for young ladies to do, and so, with family encouragement and support, she chose instead to travel with relatives or other suitable companions. In 1893, when she was sixteen, she attended the World's Columbian Exposition in Chicago, and after that she took several trips to other places in the United States and Canada.

At this time, a number of larger museums in several countries were busily rounding out their bird collections, and John Russell often accepted requests to provide specimens from the Fundy region. Sarah left the collecting of birds to the men of the family, but she could and did prepare study skins to professional standards. Challenging as her taxidermy may have been, Sarah also developed her own specialty in horticulture. As the years went by, her flower gardens grew larger and more exotic. Roses were her greatest passion, yet she was always experimenting, planting various things that were not supposed to grow in Grand Manan's climate, and more often than not experiencing the pleasure of seeing her tender plants thrive. Summer visitors at the family museum were equally delighted by the mounted bird specimens and the beautiful array of flowers nearby.

By 1903, Sarah had married William Alcott Smith, and within a year her first child, Florence Lydia, was born. Helen

Louise and Mary Alcott followed at five-year intervals. But adding family responsibilities to her other pursuits did not deter Sarah from successfully taking up still another occupation. The Moses family papers show that, as early as 1903, she had begun to write short stories and feature articles that were published on both sides of the international boundary. Under her well-known by-line, Sarah E.M. Smith, she covered Grand Manan news events for the New Brunswick papers. Her creative topics ranged over the things she knew best: gardening, famous sites she had visited, local folklore, legends and industries, and interesting accounts of birds and mammals. To improve her manuscripts, Sarah bought a typewriter and mastered its use. Eventually, she found herself looking after her father's business correspondence, as well as his growing volume of letters concerning natural history. Thus Sarah became the family secretary, recorder and historian.

Sarah, William and their children lived on Nantucket, a seventy-five acre island off Woodward's Cove, where they operated a farm and nursery for Sarah's exotic plants. In 1909, John Russell had bought Nantucket from Simeon Cheney, one of New Brunswick's first recognized naturalists. Dr. Spencer F. Baird, the explorer of the Indian middens, identified Nantucket Island in his 1869 report to the Smithsonian Institution as "the residence of Simeon Cheney, the well-known naturalist of Grand Manan, whose assistance to many American naturalists has been so often gratefully acknowledged." Dr. J. Walter Fewkes, known as the "dean of American archaeology," spent the summer of 1889 on Nantucket Island collecting marine invertebrates. His report to the Harvard Museum of Comparative Zoology opens, "Nantucket is known far and wide among naturalists as the home of Mr. Simeon Cheney." During the hundred years in which it was owned by Simeon Cheney and the Moses family, Nantucket Island served as an outdoor laboratory for marine biology, ornithology and horticulture.

The first break in the family of Lydia and John Russell Moses came in 1906 with Bedford's tragic death. Only twenty-two, he had been swept from the deck of a small sailboat off North

Head, an accident that deeply saddened his family and the entire community. He had been a friendly, well-liked chap, and his promising career had ended all too soon. Then, in 1915, Sarah's husband William died. Nearly twenty years her senior, he had been in poor health for some time. After William's death, Sarah moved back permanently into the North Head family home. Only four years later, mother Lydia died, and Sarah had all the responsibility of managing a home for her father and her brother Allan as well as her three daughters. Somehow, she managed also to continue her writing and her experimental gardening. Eventually, her writing talent enabled her to fill in for the deficiencies in Allan's education. The writing of reports, so essential in scientific endeavours, fell to Sarah E.M. Smith.

It was a remarkable family trio. Father John Russell served as the knowledgeable patron for Allan's early adventures and the later explorations he himself could have enjoyed were it not for his love of making money. Sarah served as the public relations officer and ghostwriter. Allan's field notes, gathered in his native haunts or on scientific expeditions outside the country, furnished sometimes amazing, always interesting, copy for her readers, and her report-writing enabled Allan to tell the scientific world what he had found.

THREE

Ernest Joy
and the Exotic Visitor

As A YOUNG MAN, Allan Moses put in long days in his father's business and as a fisherman. But his life was not all hard work. Once the fall and winter weather set in, fishing and work at the plant slowed down, and Allan and his father often took time off for duck hunting or collecting birds for their own mounting or for other museums. Sometimes they merely went exploring through the woodlands and fields, looking for upland birds and recording what they saw. They also enjoyed deer hunting when the short season opened early in December.

The most interesting adventures of all were the overnight trips to their own Nantucket Island, or to other small islands in the Grand Manan group. On one such excursion for ducks, Allan met a kindred soul living on Inner Wood Island — Ernest Joy. The two young men became friends at once, and their paths crossed many times in the years to come. They both liked hunting, but they deplored the waste of wildlife because of the lack of adequate regulations. Most important, they both loved birds. Allan discovered that, apart from a few of the naturalists who visited the Moses home, Ernest Joy knew more about the bird life of the Bay of Fundy than any of his acquaintances. Not only that, but Ernest was curious about wildlife everywhere and was an avid reader. Like Allan, he made his living as a fisherman.

With so many common interests to bind them together, Allan Moses and Ernest Joy developed a friendship that grew stronger with the years. They found time every fall to go hunting together, but more often than not these excursions became birdwatching trips. Even at Ernest's home the study of nature

Ernest Joy (1877-1951).

(L.K. Ingersoll)

continued. Almost any season of the year he had scores of birds coming to his feeders. Some of the chickadees and sparrows were so tame that they would eat out of his hand. Ernest and his wife, Annie Ramsdell, had no children of their own, but their home was always a place of warmth and security for their young relatives.

The nature rambles with Allan were but pleasant interludes in Ernest's working life. He was often gone for days at a time to the offshore fishing grounds. Yet, even at work, he was always on the alert for unusual birds, for transients not known in the area, or for new nesting records of species that were fairly common as summer visitors. Like the Moses family, he had been entrusted with a permit to collect birds for study, and he had already contributed several interesting specimens to the Moses collection. One of them was a northern gannet, which he collected in 1901. These birds had been uncommon in the area since 1831, when Gannet Rock lighthouse had been built on their only known local nesting site.

On August 1, 1913, Ernest spotted the greatest rarity of his career. While fishing near the South East Breaker off Machias Seal Island on the outer, southern rim of the Grand Manan archipelago, he sighted a strange bird flying towards his boat. Quickly making his fishing line fast, he reached for the specimen gun. When the bird came within range, he fired a single shot, and it fell into the sea nearby. When he got it on board, he realized he had seen nothing quite like it before. He fished no more that day, or for two days afterwards. Back home at Inner Wood Island, neighbours dropped in to have a look at the curi-

Study skin of the famous albatross — a long flight into history.

(AMNH)

osity, but no one could help with identification. As soon as possible, then, Ernest got to the main island and made his way to the Moses home in North Head. Allan, John Russell and Ernest held an exciting post-mortem.

The bird was neither a gull nor a gannet, but though it was much larger than either, it slightly resembled both of the Fundy natives. This was a real puzzle. The strange creature had to be an albatross, but as far as they knew that species had never been seen in the northern Atlantic. Yet that was what it turned out to be.

Ernest presented his albatross specimen to Allan for the Moses family museum. Under ordinary circumstances, it would have been mounted in the life-like Moses style and placed on a museum shelf for display. But for some reason Allan could never explain, they made it up as a scientific study skin that could be mounted later, and they stored it away. Study skins of birds, properly made and stored, could be preserved for long periods while still retaining most of the features present at the time of preparation. The tissues, however, would tend to dry out and lose their flexibility. Then, to mount the study skins for exhibition, a taxidermist would relax them by immersing them in sand and keeping them damp with a mixture of vinegar and water until life-like characteristics could be restored. But this albatross specimen did not stay in storage for very long. Word of it soon spread through the birding fraternity on the mainland, and leading ornithologists visited Grand Manan to inspect the rare bird from the southern part of the world.

Among the professionals who came to the museum was Dr. Leonard C. Sanford, one of the most outstanding collectors on the continent, and a member of the board of directors of the American Museum of Natural History in New York City. He wanted to buy the albatross skin, but it was not for sale. For several years, letters passed annually between Grand Manan and New York, all to the same purpose. Finally, Dr. Sanford made a second visit, during which he not only offered more money, but made a strong case that the specimen should one day become part of the American Museum's collections. As he pointed out, it would then be available for professional study by the world's most expert ornithologists. He also hinted that other unspecified benefits might come from such an exchange.

Allan still refused to sell, but he did make a counter offer. If a place could be found for him on one of the Museum's scientific expeditions, if that were one of the benefits intimated, Dr. Sanford could have the highly prized bird free of charge. The agreement was quickly made, and the albatross was soon on its way to the big city.

The American Ornithologists' Union checklist was — and remains — the authoritative reference on distribution of birds in North America. Although this albatross was collected in 1913, its description, and consequently its acceptance, did not appear in *The Auk*, the Union's journal, until 1922, when "Notes on Tubinares, Including Records Which Affect the A.O.U. Checklist" by Robert Cushman Murphy appeared. This description contributes not only to the ornithological record, but also to the ongoing dispute over title to Machias Seal Island:

> *Thalassarche chlororhynchos (Gmelin)*. Yellow-nosed Mollymawk. The first North American record of this sub-antarctic albatross is based upon a skin in the American Museum of Natural History (collection of Dr. L.C. Sanford, No. 9835) . . . It was collected near Seal Island, off Machias Bay, Maine, on August 1, 1913, by Mr. Ernest Joy, subsequently coming into the possession of Mr. Allan L.

An albatross, 7,000 miles from home. (AMNH)

Moses and, finally, that of Dr. Sanford. Seal Island is Canadian territory, and since the locality in which the bird was killed is on the international border, south of Grand Manan, the record constitutes an addition to the avifauna of both New Brunswick and Maine.

Many years later, an "accidental record" turned up documenting an albatross visit to Moisie River, Quebec, on August 20, 1885, but the Joy-Moses-Sanford bird is the first actually recorded by the Union, and it remains one of the first two known to have ventured into North American waters. There are thirteen species of albatross in the world, and this wanderer belonged to one of the nine species inhabiting the southern oceans. There are five species of "mollymawks," or medium-sized albatrosses. *Diomedea chrysostoma* (as *Thalassarche chlororhynchos* is now called) breeds in the Tristan da Cunha group and on Gough Island in the South Atlantic. Its wingspread averages six to seven feet, considerably smaller than that of the largest albatrosses. While *Diomedea chrysostoma* is a pelagic bird, living on the sea except during the breeding season, this first specimen to be recorded in North America had travelled nearly 7,000 miles from home.

An International Agreement

While Dr. Sanford and Allan Moses discussed the fate of Ernest Joy's discovery, protection-minded Canadians and Americans rejoiced over a movement toward conservation measures for the entire hemisphere. During the first decade of the present century, the governments of Canada and the United States were under pressure to introduce regulations to protect migratory birds. In the U.S.A., spring shooting was prohibited in several regions, but the two countries needed to cooperate if legislation was to be really effective. Negotiations to draw up a treaty "for protecting the birds that pass from one country to another" began in 1914. In Canada, this process meant discussions with each of the provinces and, complicating the matter still further, the British government was also involved because Canada had not yet achieved sovereign status. Consequently, it was not until August 16, 1916, while World War I raged over Europe, that a treaty was signed in Washington. Ratification was followed by enabling legislation in both countries, and thus the Canadian Migratory Birds Convention Act came into being. Though the Act has since been modified, the essential provision was a lifesaver for many species: Article II provided for a closed season for game birds from March 10 to September 1, with three and one-half month open seasons staggered according to region. Perhaps most notable of all, the Act mandated a closed season throughout the entire year on insectivorous and other birds.

Hailed by many as an enlightened step towards conservation, the Migratory Birds Convention Act was as widely damned by others. Enforcing it proved to be extremely difficult. The Conservation Commission in Ottawa had carried out the necessary work leading up to the signing of the international treaty, and enforcing the Act fell to the Parks Branch. Later, in 1947, the

Canadian Wildlife Service would be formed to take over this responsibility, and biologists specializing in wildlife would be
engaged to learn more about our natural heritage and how to
save birds and mammals thought to be endangered. But in the
meantime, in December 1918, the Parks Branch appointed
Hoyes Lloyd of Toronto as the administrator of the migratory
birds regulations under the Act. Though he was a professional
chemist, Lloyd's avocation was ornithology, and he was one of
the many who had urged positive action for conservation.

Lloyd attacked the problem on a number of fronts. One of
the first regulations, startling in some quarters, was the ban on
the shooting of ducks and geese on their nests. With little
money in his budget, he called for volunteers and appointed un-
paid honorary game wardens throughout Canada. In order to
help cover travel expenses, he allowed the wardens to keep half
the fines they collected from poachers.

On the Firing Line

One of the most troublesome areas was the north shore of the
Gulf of St. Lawrence, extending up the coast of present-day
Labrador. This long expanse of coastline, beginning approximately at Mingan in Quebec's Saguenay County, was all referred
to as Labrador, after the name of the great peninsula of which it
was a part. Although there were good harbours, much of this
coastline was barren and rock-bound, isolated and sparsely settled. Home gardens were almost unheard of and it was next to
impossible to raise domestic animals for food. Fish and sea
mammals were plentiful in season, however, and they attracted
hunters and fishermen from Newfoundland and more distant
places. Apart from that, sea birds and their eggs were the only
change of diet available. Understandably, closed seasons and
other restrictions were unwelcome.

Harrison F. Lewis, Chief Migratory Birds Officer for Labrador, was one of the first such officials to be appointed; his
manuscript history of the Canadian Wildlife Service is now held

by the Public Archives of Canada. In 1921, in cooperation with the Maritime provinces' regional officials, he set up what was known as the Labrador Patrol. Well-qualified wardens from both areas were engaged to enforce the unpopular new regulations. The officers worked on a seasonal, full-time basis, from early spring to mid-September, covering the vital breeding period for most of the vulnerable species.

Allan Moses was invited to leave the comforts of home and friends and join the Labrador Patrol. In mid-May 1923, he reported for duty at Harrington, the supply base for one 400-mile segment of the coast. He was issued a tent and other equipment, along with a supply of canned foods, and he soon established himself at his own lonely outpost. Labrador in mid-May was a cool place for outdoor living. Allan could see icebergs offshore glistening in the sun, and the wind from that quarter had a decidedly chilling effect on the temperature. Yet on most days the air was clear, sparkling and altogether invigorating, and this scenic part of Canada offered interesting possibilities for the study of nature.

The Gulf of St. Lawrence, a vast area of great natural beauty, has always been one of the great sea bird breeding areas of the world. On Anticosti, Bonaventure, and the hundreds of smaller islands, and along the long northern coast of the Gulf, nested thousands of gannets, kittiwakes, guillemots and murres, and scores of other species, including great flocks of eiders. In its northern reaches, opposite Newfoundland, the Gulf narrows into the funnel of the Strait of Belle Isle. There, the churning waters bring up food from the depths, attracting fish and birds and, in turn, men. Bonaventure and Percé Rock off the Gaspé, and the Bird Rocks in the Magdalens, had been declared bird sanctuaries in 1919, but that still left vast areas for hunters to exploit.

Allan's jurisdiction was a twenty-mile stretch of coast, including not only the shoreline but also all the little islands that had to be reached by boat. The local people were friendly, for the most part, and genuinely hospitable. The sudden approach of summer changed the terrain and the climate like magic, and had it not been for the hordes of outsized mosquitoes, Allan's experience might have been idyllic. Inevitably, he had skirmishes with poachers, most of them from outside the region, yet the mere presence of a warden was generally enough to provide security for the birds. He visited all the nesting places regularly, estimating the number of females and, later, of chicks. Exploring the cliffs to check on the great murre rookeries posed more than the hazard of a fall and broken bones. Numberless tiny parasites lived in and around the guano. These "murre ticks," as they were called locally, were not content merely to bite their human hosts, but would burrow beneath the skin. In spite of his precautions, Allan became a victim when one of them dug into his neck. He was an unwilling and often miserable host until the creature could be removed by minor surgery several months later.

In those days, winter transportation for tending trap lines and for other needs was by dog team. Hungry, half-wild and unemployed during the summer, the dogs presented a serious menace to all the little communities. When the first cow was brought to Harrington in the summer of 1922, it had to be guarded constantly. At the Grenfell Mission hospital, a flock of twenty hens had been donated; idle sled dogs broke into the pen and killed them all.

During the late summer, when fish were being cured along the shore, the ferocious creatures were put on offshore islands. In spite of being fed daily, they often gathered in packs and swam to the mainland, making their way from one island to another and destroying almost everything in sight. They became such a problem that government officials tried several times to substitute domestic reindeer as a mode of travel. That scheme never worked, and the dogs remained a nuisance until their owners could replace them with snowmobiles.

This was a difficult time of transition for all concerned. Because of the imposed protection of birdlife, the inhabitants had to change many elements of their lifestyle, from their eating habits to the way they earned their living. Visitors to the coast also had to change their ways. Before the Patrol officers came on the scene, it was said to be not uncommon for hunters to take boatloads of salted eiders out of the area. Few other North Americans had had to make such great adjustments so quickly. Diplomacy was an important part of the Labrador Patrol's responsibility in those early years of its service, but Allan could see that much good had already been done. He envisioned a time when the overall work of the Service would pay broad dividends, and better communications, improved education and increased awareness would all help to create new attitudes. Then the Gulf of St. Lawrence and the long shorelines reaching up into the Arctic could nurture the sea flocks in a relatively undisturbed environment.

The summer passed quickly, as Allan busily made his rounds and reflected on a changing land. Every week or ten days, he made his way to the post office at Harrington, eager to hear from family and friends on Grand Manan. Then came the day when something more than the mail from home awaited him in Harrington. He received a letter that would remove him from his post with the Labrador Patrol and cause dramatic changes in his life. Only later would Allan connect this letter to the strange flight of the albatross.

FOUR

The Voyage of the Blossom

*A*LLAN MOSES LEFT his assignment with the Labrador Patrol in August 1923, to take part in more exciting adventures. The unexpected letter he had picked up with his family mail in Harrington contained an invitation from the Cleveland (Ohio) Museum of Natural History to join a scientific expedition to the South Atlantic. Allan accepted the offer immediately — it was a dream come true. More than anything else, it meant recognition of his capability and an opportunity to prove himself among professional naturalists.

The Cleveland Museum of Natural History had been established in 1920. Sponsored by an enthusiastic group of citizens, a number of whom were very rich, it had quickly attracted a capable staff headed by the Director, Dr. Paul Marshall Rea. Having organized their local collections, they began to look beyond the state of Ohio for specimens and data to make the museum one of the leading institutions of its kind. Out of this desire came the decision "to investigate almost inaccessible islands and shores of the South Atlantic," of which little was then known. The expedition organizers believed that bird and mammal life on some of the remote South Atlantic islands would prove to be fully as astonishing as Charles Darwin's discoveries in the Galapagos Archipelago nearly a century before.

In this objective, the Cleveland Museum had not only the blessing but also the cooperation and support of the American Museum of Natural History. In return for a share of whatever the Cleveland Museum expedition collected in the South Atlantic, the American Museum would send the Cleveland Museum valuable specimens representing North and South America and the South Pacific islands; some of these specimens would come from the collection of Dr. Leonard Sanford, the same Dr. Sanford who had struck the deal with Allan Moses for the skin of the albatross shot by Ernest Joy in 1913.

The expedition proposal quickly won financial backing. Mrs. Dudley S. Blossom, a member of the Cleveland Museum's board, donated enough money to cover the estimated costs completely. The next hurdle was finding a suitable sailing vessel. The search proved more difficult than the organizers first expected, but finally they purchased the *Lucy R.* in Nova Scotia in mid-July 1923. The 250-ton, three-masted schooner was only three years old and had served as a coastal carrier. Taken to New London, Connecticut, she was hauled out for repairs and alterations, including sheathing her bottom with copper, to prepare her for her career change. The organizers hoped to have her ready to sail by the first of September.

Meanwhile, officers and scientists began to arrive in New London, and deck hands were recruited. George Finlay Simmons, curator of ornithology at the Cleveland Museum, had been named commander of the expedition. Kenneth Cuyler, a biologist, would be in charge of collecting, assisted by Robert Rockwell and Allan Moses as collectors and taxidermists. With Captain Emery Gray as sailing master, John da Lombe, a mariner from the Cape Verde Islands, as navigator, a cook, and college-boy sailors, the party numbered sixteen when all had assembled. Huge puncheons, once used to store whale oil, were filled with fresh water and loaded into the hold. When all the stores were on board, even the deck was crowded with supplies expected to last two years or more. Delays with all the preparations worried the organizers, but finally, the erstwhile coaster — rechristened the *Blossom* after the Cleveland benefactress — was towed downriver and out to Gardiner's Bay, Long Island. At noon on November 10, 1923, the Cleveland Museum of Natural History expedition to the South Atlantic got under way.

It had taken an appeal from Cleveland to Ottawa to have Allan, the only Canadian in the party, released from his commitment in Labrador. Remembering the agreement he had made when Allan had given him the albatross skin, Dr. Leonard Sanford had recommended Allan to the Cleveland Museum as an excellent candidate for membership in the expedition. In addition to Sanford's recommendation, Allan had a combination of skills the museum needed. Of first importance was his long experience in making fine study skins of Grand Manan birds for museums and laboratories in the United States and Canada. Rating a close second was his apprenticeship aboard the sailing vessels used in the Bay of Fundy fisheries. Seamanship was not a widely distributed ability among those aboard the *Blossom* as she headed out into the broad Atlantic, and the ship's crew as well as the scientists would have cause to feel grateful for Allan's competence.

In fairly good time the vessel entered the cold Labrador Current, but soon she passed through it and into the contrasting warmth of the Gulf Stream. For a day or two it appeared, at least to the new sailors, that they had actually embarked on a romantic cruise. That dream was shattered just after sundown on the sixth day out. With the *Blossom* under full sail, a fierce gale with slashing rain almost ended the expedition in a matter of minutes.

With Kenneth Cuyler, Allan somehow got forward and began taking in canvas. A giant sea struck the bow and nearly washed them overboard, but they hung on. A deluge rushed down the forecastle companionway, left open by inexperienced hands. A capable mariner rushed to the wheel to replace a young sailor and, with the few not overwhelmed by seasickness helping out, they eventually saved the vessel and themselves. But the end was not yet in sight. For days, gale-force winds of eighty miles per hour hounded them. Thirty-foot waves tossed them about, and the *Blossom* nearly foundered. The crew manned the pumps for hours at a time, but sea water had got into the hold, stirring up the bilge with its sickening odour. Valuable supplies were ruined, and the expensive wireless equipment was put out of commission. The daily menu thereafter consisted mostly of brine-soaked sandwiches. All hands had to sleep on deck, if they could manage to sleep at all.

It was a blessed relief when the storm finally passed, and the

Supplies being loaded onto the *Blossom* at São Tiago, Cape Verde Islands. Allan is standing at left. (CMNH)

vessel sailed into the calm of the Sargasso Sea in sunshine. This giant mass of seaweed, lying south from Bermuda nearly to the West Indies and east almost to the mid-Atlantic, provided the expedition's first opportunity for scientific investigation. Underneath the heavy carpet of seaweed, they found the tiny young of larger species such as sailfish, bonito and sunfish, and many other strange forms of life. They observed at their leisure, because the vessel was held in the mass for more than a week due to lack of wind. When the wind came up and got them underway again, they sailed in a roughly southeasterly direction and arrived off the Cape Verde Archipelago, about 400 miles from the coast of Africa, just a few days before Christmas.

The expedition's sojourn in the sunny Cape Verde Islands almost erased the horrible memories of crossing the Atlantic. The naturalists spent nearly four months exploring and making collections on the ten major islands, while the *Blossom* received much-needed repairs.

On May 8, 1924, back at sea again, Allan began one of his lengthy reports to the family on Grand Manan. On course for Dakar on the coast of Africa, the vessel was sailing in smooth sunny weather as he began his account of nearly half a year in the Cape Verde Islands. He had discovered that, while the islands had much in common with one another, each was distinct, and the people who lived on each island had their own ways of life. The people they encountered in the little villages en route to various destinations on the islands were very poor. Men and women alike wore loose gowns made of old grain sacks, much in contrast to the gay colours worn in the larger towns. Nevertheless, wherever Allan and his colleagues went, they were entertained "royally" with dancing and lively music.

Allan's letter to his family included notes about local social customs. For instance, the average Cape Verde home was one of the cheapest in the world, being built of mud and stone with walls about fifteen inches thick, and the glassless windows were merely holes in the walls. Bands of musicians accompanied both funeral processions and wedding parties. The local religious beliefs allowed multiple marriages, but the islanders explained that

Loading one of the women porters, São Vicente, Cape Verde Islands. (CMNH)

only the middle class followed the practice to any extent. The poor could not afford it, and the well-to-do got along without it. More than that, if a man took more than one wife, he was usually obliged to acquire four. Two would fight; if there were three, two would pick on the third; four assured a measure of serenity. An ordinary bride brought her family a compensation of $12, while one who wore nice clothes and could read, write, sing, dance and cook was worth $60 or more. Divorce was a simple matter, made final when the man paid the woman back an amount equal to the original bride price.

Allan spent two weeks based in Praia, the Cape Verde capital on São Tiago Island, with two of the crew as assistants. They collected over 250 specimens, including several that were new or rare: a Darwin kingfisher, "only known in these islands"; a Spanish sparrow; a weaver bird, another "native"; a glossy ibis, one of the first scientific records; and, something of a surprise, an "American" barn owl, which had never been properly described from here.

Then the expedition used São Vicente Island as its home base for two months, and Allan reported that he had already resoled his heavy leather boots twice, due to the wear from climbing the mountains and walking across miles of volcanic stone and sand. One morning, he and two assistants left São Vicente for a side trip to Santo Antão Island, a six-mile voyage. The deck of the ten-ton boat was crowded full of live pigs and goats as well as people, most of whom became seasick shortly after getting under sail. At Santo Antão, Allan and his companions engaged a guide and an interpreter. They had long since discovered that in the Cape Verde Islands, it was the women who earned the family living. Thus they found no novelty in hiring eight women porters to carry their equipment and supplies. But the performance of these porters astounded the North Americans. "I never saw such women," Allan wrote. "They would take sixty or sometimes one hundred pounds on their heads and carry it for hours at a time in the hot sun. On Santo Antão we had to climb seven thousand feet up into the clouds and the porters only rested twice. At the top, they sat down and rested, [then] sang and danced while we were all in." What Allan did not tell the folks at home but later recounted to a friend was that, once they reached the campsite on such side excursions, the women were also happy to take over housekeeping duties for a penny a day.

Allan spent time on all of the islands except Brava and Fogo, which had been assigned to other members of the party. Summarizing his work in the Cape Verde Islands, he recorded that he had made about 800 study skins, most of them in one month. Fifty-nine white-faced petrels had been prepared in a day; they had been collected by others, but due to high temperatures the work had to be shared to preserve the specimens as quickly as possible. He and Robert Rockwell, the other taxidermist in the party, had taught crew members how to skin the birds, and a few of them had become quite skilled at this delicate procedure. In total, the expedition had collected hundreds of specimens, some of them, such as the "ghost" petrel, very rare indeed. Altogether, the expedition had added well over twenty-five species to the previously-known seventy-five.

For all the hard work and often uncomfortable working conditions, the lush climate and scenic beauty of the islands left a deep impression on the Grand Manan naturalist. Some of the beautiful island valleys were watered well enough to support lush gardens, and Allan wrote of seeing his first coffee bushes and coconut palms, as well as oranges, lemons, bananas, sugar

Allan preparing specimens for shipment to Cleveland. (CMNH)

cane and wild tomatoes — a cherry-sized variety that bore its tasty fruit in clusters. In a special note to his sister, he said he was thinking of returning to the Cape Verde Islands when he got old, then marrying three or four wives who would do all the work while he relaxed in the shade. Though he made this remark in jest, it was also a compliment to the archipelago which, soon after his voyage, became a popular tourist haven and a home to many with sufficient retirement funds. Social conditions have changed since the voyage of the *Blossom* but as long as expedition members lived, they could hardly forget the inequities they saw in almost every place they visited. Child care was one example. Mothers working as porters carried their infants as well as their loads. Allan told of young mothers working in the fields under the hot sun, with their babies slung on their hips or in rough pouches on their backs. When a baby was hungry, its mother paused only briefly in her work and, he reported, pressed a breast to her shoulder for the child to grasp and suckle.

A Second Wind

The *Blossom* put into the port of Dakar on May 9, 1924. She had covered the 400 miles from the Cape Verde Islands in less than four days, a record run for that vessel. Even so, the average speed of about four miles an hour had its effect on the younger men. Although the romance of the voyage had vanished, Dakar at least meant mainland.

At that time, the city of Dakar had a population of several hundred thousand and was the capital of French West Africa. It was known as "the peanut capital of the world." Not too far inland, the storied desert country borders the coastal bush regions — rich territory for explorers and naturalists.

But, before Allan and his colleagues could start their scientific work, they had to see that the expedition's more prosaic needs were met. On a small scale, the equipment needed repair, and supplies had to be replenished. On a larger scale, the *Blos-*

som had been partially repaired in the Cape Verde Islands, but now she required extensive attention in a shipyard. In his account of the trip, the expedition commander George Finlay Simmons said that the vessel "had been badly strained in the rough passage of the North Atlantic," and that, for one thing, "considerable recaulking" was needed. Writing four years later, and commenting on the work done in New London to get the vessel ready for the voyage, Robert Rockwell noted that the overhaul and refit had been "not too brilliantly accomplished." He and Allan and the one or two others who had previous sea time had been uneasy from the first day out. Personnel changes also caused difficulties. Captain Gray was hospitalized, and a new sailing master had to be found. The young deckhands were paid off and discharged, and a new crew was engaged. Dr. Rea, the Museum Director, made a special voyage to Dakar by steamer to help solve some of the problems, and he made arrangements to ship the bales and boxes of specimens collected so far back home to America.

In the meantime, the scientists began their field work. Rockwell recorded, "We began collecting in the bay, where quite a number of birds were taken. Mr. Allan Moses and Mr. Kenneth Cuyler were the best shots on board and the most successful collectors. Much of my time was taken up in preparing the birds when they brought them to the ship." Among other unusual species, Allan brought in a rare beteleur eagle, "endowed by nature with a fierce looking head," Rockwell said, "but hardly any tail at all."

When the scientists realized that they would have time to collect some of the mammals of the region, Rockwell took charge of a safari to several inland destinations. With Cuyler and a number of assistants, Rockwell led the party on the first leg of the journey by train, and then they progressed on foot. They collected hartebeest, antelope, waterbuck, wart hog and, most prized of all, a short-maned Gambian lion, taken by Rockwell — the first of its kind brought to America. The great beast measured over eight feet in length and weighed 450 pounds. Allan missed out on that excursion, forced to nurse his disappoint-

Allan busy with his collections, Dakar, West Africa. (CMNH)

ment as he slowly recuperated from an attack of the malaria he had picked up in the Cape Verde Islands. His weakness limited him to shorter treks along the shores and marshes near Dakar.

The Cleveland Museum scientists forged excellent relations with local officials, suppliers and others, once these people understood the purpose of the expedition, and they enjoyed many courtesies that increased the success of their visit. An inland district official entertained Rockwell and Cuyler at a lavish dinner at which the menu included, but was certainly not confined to, wild guinea hen, papaya and palm salad, and several kinds of wine. The Governor-General of French West Africa invited the scientists to a party at his palace in Dakar at 9:30 P.M. on July 16, 1924; a faded formal invitation remains among the family papers, addressed to "Monsieur Moses, Membre de la Mission Scientifique du Musée de Cleveland à Bord du Voilier Américain 'Blossom'." These gustatory occasions contrasted pleasantly with the briny fare on the menu during the Atlantic storm.

After nearly five months in Dakar, the *Blossom* was ready to sail. With a former Italian naval officer as the new sailing master and the new deckhands recruited in Dakar, the expedition made

A hungry pelican being fed by Allan and native porters. (CMNH)

for the open sea about the end of September 1924. Adverse prevailing winds made the return trip to the Cape Verde Islands
last two weeks, rather than four days. There, the expedition had
to spend more time to recruit a new navigator. It was early November when the doughty little vessel could head south again,
towards the coast of South America.

By November 17, the ship was caught in the doldrums, and
until the end of the month it had hardly made a natural drift.
This dreary, depressing period finally ended and, with a fresh
breeze, the *Blossom* picked up enough speed to log "sixty to
eighty miles a day." They tried to land on St. Paul Rocks, located very close to the equator, but the strong currents and high
winds made them give up after four days. Then they paid a brief
visit to the Martin Vas Rocks, before making land about mid-
December at South Trinidad, a "Treasure Island" about 700
miles from the coast of South America. Before nightfall, all
hands enjoyed fishing in the shoal waters. The most dramatic
catch was a sea turtle that weighed about 400 pounds, providing
the expedition with its first fresh meat in forty days.

South Trinidad is about four miles long and half as wide, with volcanic peaks rising to 2,000 feet above sea level. More than one party of earlier explorers had searched in vain for two separate lots of treasure purportedly hidden by pirates, but that did not dampen the explorers' hope that they might accidentally discover this booty. An air of romance hung about South Trinidad, quite apart from the excitement stirred by the prospect of finding unusual birds and mammals.

George Finlay Simmons led the surveying party ashore, and duties were assigned to the rest of the group. Rockwell and Allan began the chief collecting chores. They set up shop in a cave about twenty feet wide by as many feet high, after first evicting a colony of huge land crabs that may have been tenants there for many generations. There the two naturalists enjoyed a month-long idyll. Though the temperatures could be much too high at times, a night draft at the mouth of their cave made for comfortable sleeping. The nearby sea was alive with edible fish, and there were birds everywhere to serve as savory meals as well as scientific specimens. Near the mountaintops, the men also found wild goats and pigs, whose ancestors had been left on the island by explorers in 1700. Unfortunately, their rugged life made the creatures scrawny and unpalatable. The man-of-war birds, noddies, petrels and a score of other species were so tame that, when the men first rowed ashore, several had come out to meet them. The collectors went out each morning and gathered a bag of birds — usually by hand — and then returned to the cave for the rest of the day to make study skins. Their joint efforts added about 600 specimens to the natural treasures aboard the *Blossom*. While their papers make no note of it, their Christmas and New Year's dinners likely consisted of broiled noddies.

After well over a year away from home port, the *Blossom* arrived at Rio de Janeiro, the crowded capital of Brazil, and once again the worrisome details of administration had to be faced. A third of the party, ill with fever or other maladies, were put in hospital. The *Blossom* too needed serious attention; she was put in dry dock for extensive repairs and refitting. Some of the sailors jumped ship to sign on with steamer crews, and they had to be replaced. The naturalists had hoped to collect some of the large sea mammals in the subantarctic, but it was too late in the winter to venture that far south. Allan had hardly recovered from another bout with malaria, and that, combined with the unpromising weather and the fact that they had had sufficient adventures for the time being, led Robert Rockwell and Allan to resign their posts in Rio. They took passage on the first steamer heading north to the United States.

Eventually the *Blossom* was seaworthy again. She made stops at St. Helena Island, where Napoleon had been detained by the British, at Ascension Island and at several small islets. The vessel finally turned towards home, and the expedition ended in June 1926 at Charleston, South Carolina. It had lasted thirty-one months, covered over 20,000 miles at sea, and had taken 13,000 specimens to enrich North Americans' knowledge about parts of the world beyond their shores.

At Home Again

When Allan arrived on Grand Manan in April 1925, after nearly twenty-one months in the South Atlantic, his family and friends welcomed him warmly. Everyone wanted to hear about his adventures, and he had a great gift for telling them all, just so long as he did not have to give a public address. In his native community he was a celebrity, and his people were proud of him. Allan's father — then seventy-three but still keen of mind and busy with his fishery interests — as well as his sister and his three nieces, had first claim on his accounts of the professional highlights of his voyage. But Ralph Griffin, a deer-hunting friend in North Head, and Ernest Joy, the Wood Island friend who had collected the famous albatross, and several other naturalist cronies also wanted to know all the details about the rare specimens he had brought back to America.

After nearly two years in tropical regions with the *Blossom* expedition, Allan took several months to readjust to the climate of the Bay of Fundy. As a gentle spring turned into summer — always the most beautiful time of year on Grand Manan — he began to respond at a quickened pace. With rest and the therapy of just being at home once again, most of the effects of malaria disappeared. Fortunately, he had little need to worry about immediate employment. Since his living expenses had been paid for the past twenty-one months and he had had little opportunity or inclination to spend his money, his payment from the Cleveland Museum was practically intact. The family export business was also flourishing under his father's direction. Demand for hake sounds had dwindled after 1919 due to Prohibition in the United States, but otherwise the economy was as brisk for John Russell Moses as it was for others in the "Roaring Twenties."

One of the first things Allan wanted to do was revisit Eel Lake, west of the Whistle Road in the North Head area, where the trout had always been larger than pan size and full of fight. They did not disappoint him. Fall came, and he and his friends went hunting, ranging the familiar forest lands from Ashburton Head to Dark Harbour looking for deer and shooting ducks at Nantucket Island. Allan began again to collect specimens for the family museum, filling in the gaps in the Fundy bird collection. Then, too, once the larger museums on both sides of the border knew he was back home, they wrote to him requesting study skins. A Canadian collecting permit enabled him to carry out this kind of work at any season of the year. Interesting letters, most of them requesting information, arrived regularly, and Sarah and her typewriter were kept busy preparing Allan's reports to mainland nature publications about rare sightings or new nesting records. It was a good life, in many ways ideal for a man of Allan's inclinations.

The *Blossom* expedition had expanded Allan's international reputation in the field of natural history. The great measure of respect he had earned from the professional friends he had made on the expedition helped to advance his career. In September 1927, he received a long letter from Kenneth Cuyler, back at his job as assistant curator of ornithology at the Cleveland Museum. "Dear Mr. Mouser," Cuyler began — an intimate greeting, for "Mouser" had been as near as the Africans could get to the name Moses. "So many times," he continued, "Mr. Simmons and I sit and talk about you and all the quaint and funny sayings you used to have and many times I have been lonesome for you." After reminiscing about shared experiences, Cuyler reported that he had been asked by the Smithsonian Institution in Washington to lead an expedition to South America, to work in the area between the Orinoco and the Amazon Rivers. It was to last four to six months and, he added, it "is primarily a relief expedition to try and locate Paul Redfern, the boy who tried a non-stop flight from Brunswick, Georgia to Rio." Cuyler closed his letter "With best wishes and kindest regards to you and your family." Later, Allan received a copy of the issue of *Natural History*, the journal of the American Museum of Natural History, containing the first of Rockwell's series of three articles about the voyage of the *Blossom*. Across the front cover, the author had inscribed: "Compliments of Robert H. Rockwell, to his old friend, shipmate and fellow adventurer." Clearly, Allan Moses had been accepted into that exclusive fraternity of Americans searching the world for knowledge of man and nature.

Late in 1927, Robert Rockwell (who had joined the staff of the American Museum of Natural History as an exhibit preparator in the mammal division) wrote to say that the Museum was planning a year-long expedition to Tanganyika and the Belgian Congo. He asked Allan if he would like to join the party on contract. This was merely an advance inquiry from a friend; if he were willing, the Museum administration would send him an official offer. Allan answered enthusiastically; working for the largest and most prestigious museum of natural history in the world, even for a few months, was an exciting prospect. He enjoyed celebrating Christmas and New Year's at home with the family after spending two festive seasons abroad, but he yearned to be on the move again. There was just time enough, before his sailing orders arrived, to clear up commitments on Grand Manan, make up new personal field kits and pack his steamer trunk.

FIVE

On Safari in Africa

On MAY 6, 1928, Allan set off on the greatest adventure of his life. This new challenge, as it turned out, would lead to outstanding personal achievements, it would cause some ornithological records to be rewritten, and it would have a long-lasting effect on the conservation movement in New Brunswick. But at the time, in spite of all the excitement and anticipation, his family was worried. Africa was still the "dark continent," and little was really known about the vast central regions where the expedition would be going. John Russell wanted to travel with Allan as far as Eastport, Maine, and Allan was pleased. Neither of them was much given to expressing affection, but they both knew that this was one way to delay the final parting. A few hours after they arrived in Eastport, they said their goodbyes at the railroad station and Allan boarded the train for the next leg of his journey. In New York, he registered at the Explorers Club, which was located at 47 West 76th Street, close to the American Museum of Natural History. That famous and sumptuous hotel catered to international sportsmen, explorers and travelling scientists, and Allan had no trouble finding like-minded people to chat with there. That evening, he dined with a wildlife photographer who had just returned from South America.

On reporting to the Museum, he had a chance to talk over old times with Robert Rockwell, and then he met Dr. J.P. Chapin, Curator of African Ornithology, who briefed him on the general plans for the expedition. Financed by a Rockefeller Foundation grant of about $150,000, it would be led by J. Sterling Rockefeller, assisted by Charles G.B. Murphy — two friends

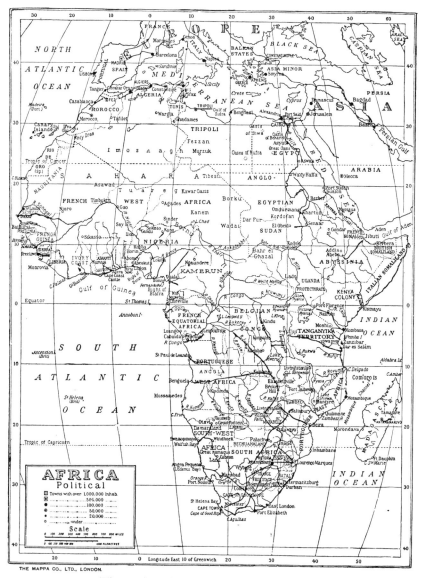

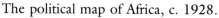

The political map of Africa, c. 1928.

who had just completed post-graduate work at Yale University. These personable young men had heard a great deal about Allan Moses and liked his style, so the three of them got on well from the beginning. Though Allan, at forty-seven, was about twice the age of his colleagues, he was young at heart, physically a match for them, and interested in the same things. Throughout their years as students, Rockefeller and Murphy had considered the Museum a place of enchantment, and now they wanted to do something worthwhile for that great institution. The expedition would also give them a change of pace before settling down in family enterprises. Of the three, Allan was the only professional, and he would be responsible for preparing specimens as well as helping with the collecting. But, before the explorers set off on their adventure, the organizers took advantage of Allan's experience as they finished the preparations for the long journey.

When the Rockefeller Foundation offered to donate money for an expedition, Dr. Leonard Sanford, still an influential board member and a friend of the Moses family, had suggested field work in the eastern-central regions of Africa to look for several very rare species, especially the rarest of them all: an elusive sparrow-sized flycatcher called the African green broadbill (*Pseudocalyptomena graueri*). Dr. Chapin, delighted with Sanford's suggestion, provided colour photos of several birds from the Belgian Congo (now mostly Zaire) that the museum needed for its collections. He thought the expedition might find the little bird with the long Latin name in the Marungu region near Lake Tanganyika. Rudolf Grauer, an Austrian naturalist, had collected the only specimen then known in November 1908. He had bought it from a native, who had found the dead bird on a jungle path "in the Akivu District of the Belgian Congo." This rarity was now in the Rothschild Museum in Tring, England. Could it be found in its native haunts? If the members of the expedition could track it down, they would enhance the reputation of the Museum and ensure that their own names would be intimately linked to a unique accomplishment.

The Museum's staff and board of trustees threw a send-off

party. Then, on June 30, Rockefeller, Murphy and Allan board-ed the Mauritania bound for London. They spent long hours en route studying the literature on African birds and mammals but, strolling the decks for their daily exercise, they also found time to watch for the great creatures of the Atlantic. At the Roth-schild Museum in Tring, after a courteous reception, they were given immediate access to the lone green broadbill specimen. They photographed it, measured it, and memorized its charac-teristics. About to search in a land where there were many small green birds, they had to prepare themselves to recognize this one at first sight. Before leaving London, they rounded out their store of supplies with everything from flash powder and darkroom materials to folding beds and first aid kits at the Army & Navy Cooperative Society's outfitting shop. When all was ready, they took passage by steamer through the Mediterranean and the Red Sea ("A fellow with my name shouldn't forget that," Allan later quipped) and down the east coast of Africa. Finally, on August 10, they reached Dar-es-Salaam, in what was then Tanganyika Mandated Territory (now Tanzania). The as-sault on the bush — their journey into the "blue" as they came to call it — was about to begin.

Before he left Grand Manan, Allan's family had told him quite clearly that, no matter what scientific challenges his party faced, he must keep a journal and, if he had any extra moments, he must also keep them up to date by letter. Allan fulfilled his family's wish, but he never once mentioned the rarest bird of all, the green broadbill, by either its common or its scientific name. His family would know by inference that the three men had suc-ceeded in their mission, but Rockefeller and Murphy had reserved the exclusive right, should they find the elusive fly-catcher, to tell the story to the world of science.

The African Letters

British East Africa
August 15, 1928

Dear Folks,

Came up from Dar-es-Salaam yesterday, having left there the night of the 13th. When I got up the next morning I saw my first wild giraffe and also a great herd of impala, as many as forty-three. There were a number of bucks and a lot of fine heads. That was some train we came up on, a wood burner and we stopped many times for fuel. It was so slow, it was painful.

The country up to this section, Dodoma, is not very interesting, some of the hills and valleys are picturesque, but the general part of it is covered with bush. We passed the native huts built of mud, sundried bricks, and thatched roofs. The land is going through a change; this is the fall of the year, leaves are falling and the grass is getting browner and more severe looking every day. We are now about three or four thousand feet above sea level; it is really cold here at night, as it well can be, remembering the mountains on the West Coast. I think the climate is fine as anything I have seen anywhere; we wear the same clothes as you wear home in the summer weather. It is a little warm in the middle of the day.

We have had great luck in getting these White Hunters, the LeMurier boys, George and Guy. They are fine chaps and are right at home in several languages, they have the Swahili at their tongues' ends, and this is valuable for dealing with the natives. I want to learn it, too, if I can, it is a simple language; fortunately, my tent boy speaks a little English. I was in Dar-es-Salaam three days, it was pretty quiet there. We are now ready to go into the blue, will start in the morning. We have a couple of motor lorries and a new Chevrolet owned by our white hunters. Will start between six and seven a.m.

Sterling Rockefeller, left, two Masais tribesmen and Allan Moses
pose on the rim of Engora Crater, Tanganyika Territory.
Masais lion spears at centre. (GMM)

Mandated Territory of Tanganyika, Africa
Boma of Embola

September 18: This leaves me well and the boys [Rockefeller
and Murphy] the same. Have had a fine hunt and got a lot of
trophies. Have been out in the blue for a month, but we have
not been lucky enough to land a lion yet. I did have the privilege of seeing six of them in one pride and was not more than a
hundred and fifty yards from them. It was about eleven o'clock
in the day; one was a handsome old male with a black mane,
which is a very rare thing to see.

We are not five hundred miles from the coast in mountain
country. Here we are about five thousand feet above sea level,
and have been from five to eight thousand feet all the month.
We hunted three weeks inside a great crater called Tokie Tokie,
about fifteen miles across. The mountains surrounding it were

about two thousand feet high. One week we were on top, eight thousand feet up. Have had much the same experience as on the Cape Verdes, with many steep climbs. On the top of the crater, we were in the clouds most of the night and next day until noon. I never experienced weather just like it, so cold and freezing at night we had to sleep with our clothes on and under three heavy blankets.

I shall never forget the sight coming down that mountain the first time out of the clouds, into the bright sunlight below and looking out across the great crater. It was literally full of wildlife; wildebeest and zebras were the most numerous, next hartebeests and Grant's and Thompson's gazelles, the beauties of the antelopes, and a few ostriches. The first thing Mr. Rockefeller shot was at the bottom: a beautiful Grant's gazelle with very good horns.

To make this camp we had to walk fifty miles with fifty porters and it took us four days to make the safari. It was hard work the first two days, but felt fine when arriving at the camp in Tokie Tokie. Of course we are seeing this country at its very best. As it is now, I have never struck a climate I like as well as this. I would not mind living here and that's the truth. But I guess when the rains come it's a different story. About the first I got at this camp was a mammoth python; it took three men to carry it in. I skinned it and got it dry; it measured nearly seventeen feet and was seventeen inches across the skin in the middle.

My best bird boy just came into the tent and said, "Umbo," which means "How do you do." Yesterday we fired him for being insulting to Mr. R. He struck him for it, that is, he slapped him with the flat of his hand. And the indignant black gentleman took his trucks and started back for Albertville [now Kalemie]. I was sorry as could be to see him go, he was the finest black for bird skinning I ever saw. He could keep me going, while any others I have had, it took two to do it. I hope he stays now. They certainly need keeping in their place. If you let one go, it makes it bad about the others, especially where we have forty or fifty around all the time as porters. It is raining and thundering and keeping it up and may last all day. So far we have not had an all day rain and this may be the first. We intended to safari today.

What a place to collect: the elephant grass has just about reached its growth. In the early morning it is full of dew, and nearly as high as one's head. More like collecting in an alder swamp, and one loses many birds. Of course all the country is not like this, only where the birds seem to be, along the river or stream valleys, and among the native shambas. Shamba means plantation where the natives grow corn, sweet potatoes, Irish potatoes, beans, mahogo (cassava) which is tapioca root. It is grown here in great quantities, dried and ground into flour.

We are doing fairly well on specimens. Counting the lot I made up in Tanganyika, we have 211. Up here in these highlands, we are getting lots of birds I never saw before. There are three Sunbirds new to me, many different Grass Warblers, and the Forest Warblers are new as well. But birds are not plentiful. One day I only got three, eleven is the highest. The boys are doing fine, they are really going to learn to be first class skinners. It is really hard for both of them to tell birds apart, but they are gaining all the time. We have picked up three new animals since coming here. Mr. Murphy got them all; he has been the only one out after them. We have to have meat for the porters and also for ourselves.

We have heard of some forests and will go to them. And I hope it will pan out, for this is our only chance to get numbers of specimens and we want a great many before leaving for America. This reminds me of a foggy day at home with rain; that cold, clammy feeling. We really should have a fire. Yesterday the three of us got caught out in the rain and went into an abandoned straw hut. We took six ears of green corn, made a fire and roasted them. I ate three. The sun broke through after a bit and we started out again and finished collecting. I got seven specimens. There were two very odd little yellow warblers with white eye rings like spectacles, a small sunbird with a crimson spot across the upper breast, two woodpeckers and a greenwinged warbler — looked like the greenwing on the other coast, but the head and throat patch were black.

September 19: Left Nbulu at 4:43 for Lake Sodis, a distance of forty-five miles, arriving there about eight. Had a cold ride in a strong wind and camped here at the Lake. The black boys went down to the lake and got water and we had a lunch of corned beef, bread, and the tea which went well after a cold ride. Had a great time getting our tents up, for the wind blew a gale. We have a new cook, a distinct advantage, he is LeMurier's boy, Josuf. Coming here last night, we saw a great many dik diks (tiny antelopes), they looked like rabbits under the auto lights. Saw three Lesser Bustards, but it was a poor place for game, considering the rest of our travels in this part of the country. But lions are certainly scarce, or very shy, for Mr. Rockefeller has never been able to get a shot at one yet, though he has been making a great try for them.

September 20: Got around about six this morning and went down to the Lake, shot a couple of ducks and a francolin and came back to the tents and got my breakfast. I then shifted to the other camping site, about a couple miles to the south. Truly, first and last, we have seen vast numbers of birds, as well as a great variety in this country, but I have never seen anything like this. Here there are doves, ducks, geese and small birds. The song birds and doves are here by the millions; the noise of their wings can be heard several hundred yards.

I saw the first hippos today, there were four of them puffing and blowing like whales and grunting occasionally. I also saw the first wild live leopard and was nearer to him than I liked. I was within fifty yards and had no gun, he was lying under a large thorn tree, not a half a mile from our tents. I came back and told Mr. R. and we went out but did not see him, he had faded away. But we got a little Nile Goose and a couple of Guinea fowl, the latter are very plentiful here, and the francolins, too. This country is quite level and almost clear of bush.

September 21: Got out early this morning and went after a kill as bait for vultures. I went about four hundred yards from the camp and sat down behind some thorn bushes. Within a hundred yards were four giraffes and I watched them some time, they were feeding off the tops of small trees and they took no notice of me whatever. I was there about twenty minutes when I heard a herd of wildebeests coming, and they walked right up within a hundred yards of me. I fired at the leader with my Winchester .405, using a soft-nose bullet and he dropped like a stone. I came back to camp and sent one of the black boys back to watch and keep the vultures from devouring the kill, for an animal like that lasts but a short time among the thousands of those hungry birds.

I got my breakfast and then Mr. R. and I went out to try our luck with vultures over the kill, that is, I meant to get pictures and also to get a couple to make up for specimens. But they would not come near while we were there. They came out and sat on the ground about two hundred yards from the bait, but that was their limit. We came near to getting a picture of an impala only, but as is generally the case, a native came along just in time to scare it.

September 22: I started this morning at 5:30 to try and get a vulture off the remains of the wildebeest that the hyenas had left, but when I arrived just a little after light, you would never know there had been bait there. A few vultures sat around in the trees, but one could not get near them. So I looked around over the plains about two or three miles from camp. I had a native with me carrying my rifle. We saw a pair of bustards and I fired a couple of shots at the male but did not get it, but we gave him a close call. So I went and tried another long shot at another one, and got it, at a hundred and eighty-eight paces. I also made up a skin with Mr. R.'s help, and it is a fine specimen. This is the country where game exists in great numbers. Mr. R. shot an ostrich this afternoon, so my job will be cut out for me tomorrow. He and LeMurier went out in the car on the road we came in on; they found three birds and got one.

October 30: This finds me in Mbuguwa. The boys [Rockefeller and Murphy] left here on the twenty-first and were going to be gone ten days. In the meantime the rains have started. It began three nights ago, and in this old black soil I tell you it is muddy, making the roads nearly impassable. The cars going by here from Dodoma to Arusha and Nairobi had to have twenty natives to shove them through; the cars were up to the hubs. There was a party of four cars here at the rest camp last night from Arusha, going to Dodoma. Another party was from a mission nearby, going through to Dodoma to meet the Bishop of the Church of England, who was on his way to their station.

There was also a family car here last night from Durban, South Africa, a man and his wife and three children. They had been seven weeks on the journey and were nearly worn out, and looked it too. They were going to Nairobi. They had a new Chevrolet, had taken the top off and fitted it up like a sleeping car, with places for five.

Well, I must say in passing, the days are pretty long here now since the boys went and I am alone. One can't buy meat, so in a way, it keeps me busy supplying the black boys and myself. I shot a good many birds for the purpose. There is a large dove here that is simply delicious, and a large wild pigeon that is fine eating. The Greater bustards and the two species of lesser, are here and we find the latter a good bird for the table.

So far, this has been nothing but a sporting trip in this spot, as there is nothing here the museum is interested in but vultures. And it's practically impossible to get near them. Although I did get one with the rifle. I have sixty specimens, of different varieties, I have collected to kill time. I fancy they will be able to make good use of them at the museum.

Apparently the rains have not set in for good, for yesterday and today up to twelve o'clock it is still fine. The weather is entirely different from the West Coast, the rains here remind me of our weather at home, the rain begins with a strong wind that goes down as it continues to rain.

There is a Catholic Church or mission very near here, and yesterday I went out to call. The priest is an American German and a splendid chap. He gave me a lot of vegetables out of his garden and I mounted a specimen for him, and we were both pleased. In the afternoon we went out in their motor lorry and the priest shot two bush pigs, but game was scarce. His assistant, who is of Alsatian French descent and nice too, got only a long shot at several impala and missed. The Father then got a chance at a bush buck at a close range and missed it. He took a second shot and this time he made it alright, but the buck leaped into the thick thorn bushes and could not be found. I had a fine visit and I found both the Fathers good sports and fine men.

November 4: Well, this is one beautiful day down here in this great valley. The hot wind now at two o'clock is making whirlwinds like before the rains, it has been dry now for four days and dusty as ever. These little whirlwinds take the dust up to the clouds, and one sees as many as half a dozen at a time going toward the mountains on the West side. The East side is quite low with scattering hills. I saw the top of a large crater at Engora, also Mount Mero and the top of famous Kilimanjaro over a hundred miles from here. This is the only time since we arrived here that we have been able to see any distance. The natives had been burning the grass and all the country has been on fire. The first two days' rain put it all out and the atmosphere is clear at last.

I saw the first scorpion two or three days ago. I have seen four centipedes; they seem to be the most dangerous, at least the black boys fear them the most. Was out after birds again last night with the gunbearer, Cetambo and the porter, "boss" Jacques. I got five specimens and there were many ducks there. The five I got were much like our bluebills and not unlike them in habits. They are very good eating.

December 2: Left Mbulu reserve this morning for the town of Mbulu ten miles away. We were hunting in the reserve for elephants. Mr. R. got a very large elephant, but it did not have what they call large tusks. One weighed fifty-seven pounds, the other fifty-three. Got a leopard in one of the gun traps that we had set with a live goat. This is not as cruel as it sounds, for there was no possible way of the leopard getting the goat, though I will agree it must have been an uncomfortable night for him. Guy LeMurier, two of the black boys and myself skinned the leopard. It was a large female, six feet long, with a fine skin. Packed up camp and started with forty porters at eight o'clock and arrived at Mbulu at noon. The reserve is a wonderful place, a typical piece of African forest, for it was a reserve when the Germans had this country.

I got five vultures and a nice lot of mice, and I think I have two very rare squirrels, very small. I also have a Guinea fowl of the forest type, with a feather crest, something I have never seen before, and another species of the large hornbill, also new. I had a hard time to get them dry. We were up there five thousand feet on the top of the escarpment, where it rained every day and every night as well.

December 3: Was in Mbulu all day, had Mr. Robinson, the district officer, or D.A. as they call him here, down to have a game of bridge last evening. He turned out to be a fine fellow; he got us porters and we had no difficulty going where we liked. He made the Mbulu boys go down the escarpment to Mbuguwa and it is nearly impossible to get porters to do it, for they get fevers down there. The walk down is fourteen miles. Guy LeMurier and I walked it in four hours. Mr. R. and Mr. Murphy stayed in Mbulu to have a game of golf. But they are great walkers, they got in at the bottom of the escarpment within a few minutes of Guy and me.

The rains have struck that part of the country, but even so and in spite of rainy weather, this is, I honestly think, one of the finest spots in the world. Especially Mbulu. The weather here is like the finest of our summer; in the middle of the day it's a little warmer, but at night one can use two woollen blankets nicely. Mosquitoes are rarely seen, and fever unknown. Lucky for all of us, we have not had a single case of fever among us.

December 4: Left Mbulu this morning at ten o'clock for Mbuguwa. Guy and I started ahead of the porters and walked to the top of the mountain, twelve measured miles, in three and a quarter hours. This escarpment is the West side of the Great Rift Valley, and is just three thousand feet down to the bottom of the zigzag path. We tented there at the bottom last night. It is a lovely walk up hill and down dale, for the country is rolling all the way, and all the edge of the escarpment is wooded with its great valleys and hills. From Mbulu flats looking at the escarpment, would remind you of looking across from North Head to Ohio Hill, only the hill here is three thousand feet high and the clouds are on it all the morning until nine or even ten o'clock.

December 5: Left the bottom this morning for the native village of Mbuguwa in the motorcar, had everything packed up, and forty porters followed us, we went to the rest camp, got there early and the porters arrived about noon. I am glad we left that part of the country, for Mbuguwa is a fever spot, and the mosquitoes are there now. They are not so bad in the dry season. Stayed there overnight and got no word of elephants. So we started for Dodoma.

December 6: Left Mbuguwa for Condor Angia, on our way to Dodoma. Left in the morning early, but hired an Indian with a truck to take our baggage to Dodoma, a two days' trip by car, ninety miles to Condor Angia, one day's ride and ninety-seven more to Dodoma. The first day was not very interesting, but from Condor to Dodoma was by all means the finest trip I ever had in a car. Up hill and down dale, over another escarpment covered with a tropical forest, hung with the long lichen that we used to call "old man's whiskers." It was rolling country and in every way a memorable trip. But strange to say we saw no game either day, only one dik dik and a bush pig. Arrived here yesterday, and will have a hunt for Great koodoo (a large grayish-brown antelope with white markings), one of the rarest of African animals. We hope to start shortly for the Congo. The rains have started here, too, it rained this morning but not long. They are looking for a downpour soon but we don't want to see it for a few days. The game clears out in the rainy season.

Before leaving Dodoma we paid off Guy, who was leaving us there. Both he and George, his brother, were good fellows and have been a great help to us in Africa. We left the hotel at Dodoma the 11th at two o'clock in the morning, and Guy came to bid us goodbye and good luck. He was with us four months and we all like him very much. Both were interesting chaps; they had spent fifteen years in India and spoke the Indian language like they were born to it. As there are many Indians here who do most of the trading in this part of the country, they could talk to them to our advantage. We have bought our supplies from them many times on this trip. So, we are going to look for koodoo without benefit of local help.

December 9: We are here at Dodoma again; this is the place where we started our first safari into the bush, and is a twelve hour run on the train from Dar-es-Salaam. It is strange that I never got my mail. I was sure I would get a letter here, but there was nothing. I suppose you didn't have the right address. Am perfectly well and have had a great time.

This is one of the finest climates in the world! Since coming here, I have talked with some of the old world wanderers, for here is the spot one finds them. Men from sixty to seventy years of age, many of them retired officers from the British or the Indian armies. Great sports. Ivory poachers or something else mighty interesting. They come here and get a piece of land and finally settle down.

In a big game hunt there is little time for anything else. I have a few specimens, but there was so little here that the museum really wanted. There is a lot of game, but not since the rainy season started. It has all scattered and one doesn't see so much of it. We have been very high up in mountain country. At the great crater of Engora, we were as high as 9,000 feet and up until yesterday were not lower than 6,000 feet. Up in that altitude it was really very cold at night, but beautiful in the day. In the crater there were many of the famed natives called Masais, who kill lions with spears. They are workers in iron, make wonderful spears and they know how to use them. I tried to get a spear to bring home, but they could not be induced to part with one, any more than one of us would part with a favourite gun.

I have seen a great many kinds of African game. A strange experience was a pride of several lions, all males, one with the beautiful black mane. I saw a leopard too, a beautiful sight. The birds are gorgeous and of many kinds. I hope you have the beautiful little sunbird I sent, one of the finest I have seen.

I have been many miles from post offices on this trip, but have tried to get a letter home whenever possible. I am sending the new addresses, so write me as soon as you receive this. I will send my journal in a week or two. Have walked in the last three and a half months over five hundred miles; it will be in my diary. The first long trip to the crater was one hundred miles and we walked it in four days.

It is spring here now, the trees are coming into leaf, the birds getting their summer dress, and nesting. I suppose by the time you receive this there will be lots of snow around at home. It is very stuffy here at Dodoma, much hotter than where we were hunting. I don't know when we will start now as the rainy season has caught us. It is very hard when the country is saturated with water.

We may not start into the Congo until April. I trust this will find you all well and with kindest regards to the friends and best wishes for a happy Christmas and New Year.

January 2, 1929: Left Kedete yesterday where we were hunting greater koodoo, we are now in Killingdale, about thirty miles from Kyigome, which is one of the towns on the railroad to Dar-es-Salaam. The boys found it pretty hard hunting koodoo, they are so rare. Mr. R. got a fine head, about fifty-seven inches, and Mr. Murphy had a chance at a couple but missed. They saw them every day, that is young and female. I saw them myself, they are beautiful animals weighing about three hundred pounds, with very long necks. The spiral horns are very good looking. The one Mr. R. got had two turns and a half, about four inches at the base. Mr. Murphy got a buffalo, and this is some feat, as they are as dangerous an animal as one can meet in this country. Spent Christmas at Kedete, stayed in camp all day, had a Guinea fowl for dinner, and that is just as good as any turkey; they are delicious.

Yesterday, New Year's Day, we spent most of the time walking here. We are really now on our way back to Dodoma and later to the Congo.

January 3: Rained this morning, hard until nearly noon. Mr. R. walked to Kilosa with his boy, and is going to take the train to Dar-es-Salaam to get us some more supplies before leaving for the Congo. It was still raining when he left, and the walk was about fifteen miles. Mr. Murphy and I will go to Kilosa tomorrow, then on Saturday Mr. R. will send a truck for us. I tell you this is a job, moving all the time. But in this country living in a tent is fine. I think now we will be out of here before the bad rains start.

Was out last night with Mr. Murphy after meat. Had my Winchester out for a bush pig, saw lots of them but did not get a shot. Mr. M. got a reed buck, so now we are fixed for meat for a couple of days. It would last longer only the weather is getting hot and it will not keep so well. I never saw so many insects in Africa as there are here. They don't seem to hurt, or even bite much. I had to build a fire before supper, they made for the blaze and that was the end of the most of them.

January 7: Arrived here last night at Dodoma on a freight train. Could not get a chance on the one last night as it was so crowded with people going home from Dar-es-Salaam, where they had been for the Christmas holidays.

Our last camp was an interesting one. There were no mosquitoes, no ticks, and a nice comfortable roaring of lions every night, an occasional stampede of game through the camp that did no harm, and endless howling of hyenas of course. One lion was a regular old sport, he never did neglect us while we were there, coming very near our tents and we used to hear him every night. I shall never forget that noise.

Out to Kedete at Kilosa we stayed with the game department

officer. Mr. Swinerton is the head of the department, and Capt. Fairweather is in charge of game administration. I was glad to meet them, they were most hospitable and entertained in a way that left nothing out. We got a truck to take our camping outfit to Killingdale and Capt. Fairweather took the three of us out in his car. One thing I can say for the English people here, they have used us fine. Truly, they have put themselves to considerable trouble to help us out. When Mr. Murphy and I came into Kilosa we were taken back up to the hills again and Mr. Harvey, another game officer, took charge of us and let us have Capt. Fairweather's house to stay in, with our personal black boys, too. We had a bath and were comfortable as could be, but on account of the crowd we missed the train that night but made it alright the next night.

Arrived here last night around midnight and got to bed in the hotel at two o'clock. This is where I should have my address. I might have a chance to get a letter, not a line from home yet. Of course every letter has gone to Albertville in the Belgian Congo. We are now going to the Marungu Mountains, it is the largest place we have to collect and we will be there three months. Don't worry for we will be miles from a post office and will not be able to send letters until we come out. We will go back to Albertville when we come out of the hills.

Before I forget it, I must tell you about the Prince of Wales and the Duke of Gloucester. They hunted from the very camp we were in at Killingdale, and under the same tree, after koodoo. They also stayed here in this very hotel (George's) in Dodoma. They gave the Prince and his party a great dance. This place is run by Greeks, there are a great many of them in this part of the country.

We are now trying to organize our equipment, and it is quite a job. Mr. Murphy and I have been at it two days and not through yet. We are getting boxes for all the skulls and horns, and I am certainly having a hard time to save the stuff from the various bugs that infest this country. I have painted all the skins today with a special solution and I hope they get home safely. This is surely the place for creeping things, but as far as snakes go I have only seen about four or five in all the time we have been here, and we have been out in the blue ever since we arrived.

January 10: This is a memorable day. Mr. R. came back from Dar-es-Salaam early this morning with my letters, dated August 5, August 19, September 1 and September 22. Now I expect to get the others in Albertville in the Congo and we will be there soon. I may send another address by wire in a day or two. I notice what you say about this climate — you are right. It is wonderful. I never was in such a place in my life. Some of the letters were badly shaken, but they arrived safely and that's the main thing, but use heavy envelopes next time.

I have the box of birds ready and will send them now with all the trophies belonging to the boys. We are leaving for Kigoma on the East shore of Lake Tanganyika for several days, then we are going down to the Marungu Mountains on the southern edge. I am glad to say at this writing that I am well, and the boys too. These last few days have been wonderful, they remind me of the best of our September days at home, with beautiful white clouds rolling up from the southeast.

Next day — well we had a day of it! We packed the skins and heads, I am sending home a large piece of rhino hide, enough to make a table top — it takes a high polish and is used and much liked for that purpose. I am sending another zebra face, and a cane made of rhino hide, the big one Mr. R. shot, and a Kaboko lash that the Germans use for discipline. This shipment is going to taxidermists in Yonkers, New York, who will forward my packages to you. I have only one regret in leaving this place, and that is, that more of our collecting could not be done here. I am glad to say I had nine of the vultures to send. I also put up one of the Greater bustards, a bird they did not have in the museum. But it's the very devil to make specimens! I made up a lot of things to fill in time, but I fancy they will be able to use it all, as I had such a good chance to select the very best, and we have been in this country so long I was able to get birds in the best of plumage.

The waterholes in the river were small and hundreds of heads of game came there every night to drink. I think by the actions of the vultures that the lions made a kill there every night, too, but there was never one of them visible in the day time. There is a hyena woo-oo-ing now, this is quite a place for them. I can imitate them exactly. I often give the black boys a start in the bush, but it does make them laugh. We saw twenty lions the night the three were collected. Eight young were on the bait at one time. One can never find them in the daylight, they are very wary and shy, more so than any of the animals we have collected. When you hear from me again it will be from the Belgian Congo. Best regards and good wishes to all the friends.

Allan L. Moses

SIX

Life in the Jungle: The Quest Achieved

ALLAN CONTINUED TO write to his family and keep his journal as the expedition pressed on.

In The Marungu Mountains
Central Africa

Dear Folks,

April 24, 1929: Was out this morning, but only got a small finch that is new, and a couple of medium-sized ring-necked Doves; the male will be included in the collection. There seems to be a lot of birds here, most of them common to our collection, still we are picking up quite a few of the specimens we need. Mr. R. brought in five more this morning and Mr. Murphy is not in yet. I think our total will be over five hundred.

This is nearly the end of the rainy season and I will be glad to see the last of it. It is the season for insects that flourish beyond the power of anyone in a temperate zone to even imagine. Our boxes are here and tomorrow will see us "on the war path" again. We are now on the stretch for Moba on Lake Tanganyika.

May 5: Left Ketendwe this morning about eight o'clock, and were about six hours arriving at Mukuli. It was a very good safari with about forty men, women and boys as porters. We are now within two days of Moba on the shore of the lake. Our collecting in the Marungu plateau region southwest of the lake is about done and the biggest searching job in Africa is (nearly) over. We did not find the rarest species on our list; they were not here at all. However, we have a good representative collection, though I saw very few song birds that had not been collected. We have walked many miles since we came to Africa, enough to go across America, and I am proud of what we have done thus far.

Travel books and travellers' stories to the contrary, I have seen very few "jungle highlights," but now I am going to tell you something that may chill your blood!

It was May 2, the night we arrived at Ketendwe, in fact. It was very dark, and Mr. Murphy was still out for meat, while Mr. R. and I were sitting in our tent talking about going home and the route we would take. Suddenly, we heard a noise outside that sounded like a motor boat, a slight growl, and a boy crying, "Simba! Simba!" (lion! lion!) and the rush-off with the body. This all happened in a few seconds and the poor victim was gone in the tall grass, a meal for three lions, a large male, a female and a cub. It made my blood run cold to think of this happening within thirty or forty yards from our tents; we had even heard the terrible wallop that dispatched the unlucky black.

We grabbed our guns and rushed out with the gasoline lanterns. All there was to tell the tale were the great tracks in the tobacco bed by the side of the hut, where the boy had been sitting. They call everyone boys here, but this one was full grown, though still young, able to carry a load of at least a hundred pounds.

This happened about seven in the evening. Next morning Mr. R. and Mr. Murphy followed the tracks about a mile from town and off the main road. Mr. R. ran into one of them, and was within twenty yards, but the lion was in grass eight feet high. It was lying under a tree and got up, growled a little and walked off. The two men decided it wasn't worth the game to follow man-eating lions in tall grass. They then decided to put out one of the Rowen antelopes Mr. Murphy had brought in the night before, and build a mechan (blind) in a tree and sit up all night for the beasts. They did so, but still with no success;

one of the lions came and circled around the area two or three times and left.

All we were able to locate of the poor victim were two splintered leg bones and the skull licked out clean. A most terrible fate.

We met a French district officer in Doyle who gets papers from Europe. He was the first white man we had seen for over two months and a half, and he told us of the terribly cold winter in America and Europe. The only effect in these mountains was floods of rain; he has been in Africa sixteen years and had never seen anything like it. It rained in Marungu plateau and the surrounding mountains twenty-six days in February.

Well, in two or three days we will be over the biggest job of our expedition. I, for one, need a rest as I have certainly been going (steadily) on this trip.

On Board S.S. *Baron Dhams* Bound For The Northern End Of Lake Tanganyika

June 7, 1929: We left Kigoma yesterday. I mailed your letter the fifth. I thought this steamer was sailing that day but did not get off until the sixth. One never knows when they will start in this country. The steamers belong to "The Grand Lake Co.," a big firm both here and in the Congo. The ships burn wood and were in a little bay all night to get fuel. The natives cut it and carry it down to the steamer on their backs and are hired by the company to do it. Everything burns wood, and many natives are employed to cut it for steamers, trains, hotels, etc.

Truly, this lake reminds one of the ocean, only, generally speaking, it is smoother, but when it does blow hard it gets very rough. We have been lucky as we have always had beautiful trips. So far this morning it has been blowing quite hard. There are so many passengers, we could not get rooms, so had to use our cot beds on deck. The food is unusually good. We left Kigoma at ten o'clock yesterday morning and will not see that spot again. It is really a fine little place and beautiful at this time of year, a wonderful climate. There is an enormous population of natives, and only a handful of whites who are all government officials.

Well, this time in Kigoma we met an interesting Englishman. He was an aviator in the war. His mission here is to get movies of gorillas. He went ashore at Baraka and is going to spend a month in the forested mountains, two or three days safari from the village. He has done a lot of this kind of work and has also tried to get the gorillas before. We found him very interesting and a good fellow. His name is Charles S. Bird. And I was truly sorry to see the last of him.

June 9: Arrived here at Uvira yesterday. This is a large town of natives and not a great many whites. It is beautiful here, under the mountain, near the foot of it. The mountains run up several thousand feet with numerous peaks. The main road runs along the shore of the lake. This is Sunday and we hope to get away tomorrow, probably in the afternoon. We are in another Greek hotel; the great trouble with these places is the quantity of olive oil they use on everything, entirely too much. We have to go quite a way in an auto truck before we safari.

June 11, Lrounge: Left Uvira yesterday. About three miles out the black driver got the car off the road as something was wrong with the steering gear, so we had to wait two hours or more until a boy could take a note back to the company and get another truck. We transferred our luggage and got here just at dark. This is the Ruzizi Valley, it is thickly populated with natives. They use the tree cactus for their cattle bomas (corrals) and also for the enclosures around their houses for protection against leopards and lions. We are very close to the mountains; we hope to find some very rare birds and if things go well with us we ought to be collecting in a few days. The country here is hazy as it was in the crater. It rained nearly all night. We are thirty miles from Uvira now in a little hotel run by a German Belgian and his wife.

June 16, Lemera: We are here at last, having arrived the four-teenth. We are now at the Swedish Mission and have reached an elevation of 5,400 feet. Had quite a hard safari, but now we are within a four hour walk of the top of Mount Kandashomwa, where we will hunt for a rare bird, one of the most important on our list. At present, we are hung up for men to work as por-ters. May get them tomorrow.

Was to church this morning, the sermon was Swedish and in-terpreted into Swahili by a young Swedish woman, with the other (local) language interpreted by a black boy. There were about sixty blacks in the church, a Swedish man and his wife, along with our party.

We are staying in the local school building. From the door I can look out on the market place for the surrounding country, about a half mile away, where a few hundred natives have gath-ered. The market days are interesting. Natives come from miles around once every five days. They bring goats, cattle, bananas, corn and all the produce they raise. They butcher the animals right on the spot, and cut them up for sale.

Looking out the window on the west side of the school, we can see the mountain where we are supposed to find the rare species. It seems the last collector here who, by the way, failed to find it, gave the missionary a picture of the bird. The padre now tells us he has seen it up there which, of course, is very en-couraging to us.

I think we will have men to go with tomorrow. The officials have taken men from the crowd who come to the market, but it seems they are reluctant to be employed. The Sultano (chief of the village) sent his son and his police for the recruiting job and they brought ten natives here all tied together. One of the po-licemen had been badly cut with a spear, in the melee. But they seemed satisfied enough, and will make good porters when they are once on the road.

I like the appearance of this country, it's really beautiful and interesting, too. We are surrounded by great mountain peaks, and foothills. The mountain that is our objective is 10,000 feet, capped with bamboos and cold enough to be uncomfortable.

But here in the foothills the climate is beautiful, just right, neither too hot nor too cold. In fact, it's very much like Mbulu, Tanganyika Territory. This would not be a bad place to make a permanent home. We came up here out of the great Ruzizi Valley, which runs north from Lake Tanganyika and is very large, I should judge ten miles wide, and far as we could see was full of native villages.

This is a very fertile tract and the natives have fine gardens. I noticed lots of corn (muhindi) but it is nothing like our own, generally small and irregular, that is, the ears are not uniform and it is pure white. Another plant used in their gardens everywhere is millet (mtama). This is prepared with a mortar and pestle, made into a kind of thick pudding, then they gather it up in their hands, and make it into a ball and eat it. The corn is ground in a mortar, too. We would come up to a village and ask the Sultano for corn meal (muhindi unga). Usually there would not be a quart prepared in the village, but soon the pounding of the pestles could be heard all over the place. Usually each woman brought her own, anything from a quart to half a bucket. She would put the vessel (kitunga) down and sit down beside it. We waited until they all came in and were sitting in a long line, when one of the boys started at the end of the line and paid them off, so many francs a kilo. The meal was finally poured out on a large cloth, or on a smooth clean place on the ground, and was measured out a kilo to a man (this was for our porters). The native boy who had charge of safari did this. The porters cook their own food, sometimes one man alone, but generally a number of them together.

It is a shame there is now so much smoke one can't see anything; the natives are burning the grass every day, and will be that way until the rainy season comes again. We are just now at the edge of the bamboo forest, small compared with those on top, for the trees up there are four or five inches through and run up forty or fifty feet. This is the first time I ever saw a forest of bamboo. Just think, giant "grass" one can walk through, like a birch forest.

I was glad that we were able to get this rest today. I darned a pair of socks this morning, and I am going to make some fishballs [fishcakes]. We received the Grand Manan fish at Albertville, and it will be a treat.

The fishballs turned out a great success, but made me think of home. Everybody liked them and we plan to have them every Sunday as long as the fish lasts.

Two of us just finished labelling our week's birds, and we have twenty-four. They very kindly sent us a few vegetables from the Mission this afternoon. There did not seem to be very much we could do for them in return, but they had never been able to get much game where the Mission is located, so one day I had the good luck to get a little duiker. I immediately prepared it and sent it down by one of the boys. This was a great treat for them, as it is one of the smallest antelopes and delicious.

This mountain collecting has everything else beaten, and I think the birds will be interesting too, as there has been no collecting done here for many years, and never done thoroughly as we hope to do before we leave. We have a month to spend on this hunt and will leave nothing out to get the birds if they are here.

June 30: Sunday again and another beautiful morning. I am sitting outside the large bird skinning tent, the sun is warming and feels good after the chilly night. Am getting a very good view of the mountain, for the rain yesterday put out the fires, or at least cleared up some of the smoke. We are still at the second camp, 7,600 feet. But we plan to go up to the top next week, 9,000 feet. We will not camp on the very summit, which is around 10,000 feet and will be very cold up there. We will probably find it freezing at night.

I had a rather unpleasant experience out in the rain yesterday, up about another 1,000 feet. We were among the clouds and then to help matters the rain came pouring down. We got under a large tree and did not get wet, but were nearly frozen. Strange to say, the boy curled up beside me and went to sleep, while I was too uncomfortable to do anything but sit and shiver. Then we were wet through coming home, the ferns were all loaded with water. (Ferns here are regular trees, six feet tall.) It is always clear in the morning, but the clouds gather around the peak and obscure everything about ten o'clock.

The Mission people sent us up an English newspaper one day last week. It seemed good to see one again. When I think of the long distance between this place and civilization, and of what might happen before we could ever hear a word of it, it gives one a queer feeling that is worse even than the isolation. We did not get anything very rare this week and I feel sure there is nothing more here. We have a number of interesting birds though.

One certainly needs a rest after climbing these great hills all the week. This is truly the hardest collecting I ever did, but also the most interesting. It is the first time I ever collected in a mountain forest and a tropical forest at that. I was lucky enough to get an interesting specimen last week, a monkey, it made a fine skin and I will bring it home.

Just a year ago today we left New York. I had no idea after a year's travelling the same date would find us in the middle of Africa and only half the job accomplished. I thought we would be on the other coast anyway. You might wonder how we fare for three meals a day away up here. I don't know how they manage it, but the Britishers have the matter of tropical butter solved. They put it up in Bombay in pound tins, and when open never changes in either taste or appearance. In the warmest weather it never gave up and became greasy, but always fine and simply delicious. Lipton's tea has followed us across Africa. It's the best in the world. Canadians say they can't get any good tea since the war — well, I see where Lipton has a chance to add a few millions to his fortune. Of course we have Irish potatoes as well as all the sweet potatoes we want; once a week we have sent the boys down the mountain for a goat and six or seven chickens. We have had good bread right along; for yeast they use the native beer (pombe). As soon as we make camp the cook gets busy and starts the bread; the boys dig a hole in the ground and make a roaring fire. When the dough is ready the fire is lifted out of the hole and a gasoline tin inserted; the loaf is slipped

Allan with kori bustard, collected in East African grasslands. (GMM)

into the tin, the cover is fastened down, and presently we have some of the best bread ever tasted anywhere. These English trained cooks are clean as can be.

We like the goat meat too, but in a game country the meat problem is solved for both the black boys and ourselves. All the antelopes are fine, especially the smaller ones and the little duikers that weigh about forty pounds are delicious. We have had wonderful Buffalo steaks, while the buffalo tongue is about the choicest cut of any of the game animals. Through Tanganyika Territory we had ducks for weeks at a time, to say nothing of Guinea fowl, they were our favourite dish and to my mind were superior to turkey which it resembles; I suppose the fact that they are both pheasants accounts for it.

In some ways this hunt is discouraging, hunting for a needle in a haystack would just be a joke compared to this. We are hunting for a bird supposed to be at the north end of this lake, at least it was a longer time ago than I like to remember, and nobody has seen it since. If we run into this one, it will be pure luck. I don't believe the man from the Mission ever saw the bird as there is a warbler the same colour, but smaller and he has mistaken it for the one we want. The protective colouring of birds has been carried to the limit in this country. I have never seen anything like it, it is quite possible to look right at a bird and not see it. The tropical forest has more shades of green than one can ever imagine. It makes a cover for birds that could not be improved unless they were absolutely invisible.

Just finished labelling specimens and have thirty this week. We consider this very good, as the birds here are shy and scarce as well. This is just about sunset and when the sun finally sets we have to get our sweaters on at once. But it's no use talking, this place is really beautiful in the daylight.

The natives are still burning the grass of the lower slopes; in some places it nearly reached our tents. The burning is a big job with the natives and a necessary one, the grass grows twenty-five feet and will average twenty. When the rains start, the tender new grass makes the best pasture imaginable, and the fires burn up millions of poisonous insects, as well as many others that annoy one and make life a burden. It clears the country of snakes, too, a blessing that only people who have lived here can appreciate.

July 7: Well, another week gone *and we have not seen the bird yet.* I thought I saw one yesterday. The boys got a specimen each of a rare grass warbler and I only got one of the more common ones, plus a shrike. We are now up to our last camp, 9,000 feet. We have been moving our camp by easy stages, and in that way we have become acclimated as we progressed toward the top of the highest mountain we will collect on this trip.

We came up here the fifth; the day before I got a rare nest of a flycatcher and one egg. It was one of the most interesting I have found. It was located in an elbow of a vine overhanging a brook and everything in sight was covered several inches thick with moss, the nest was placed in this and made of it too, and lined with delicate roots like tiny black threads. The whole place was beautiful in a deep ravine, in shade like a deep twilight, and silent but for the murmur of the brook.

This is Sunday again, and glad to get a rest. We just finished dinner and had some more of the fishballs made from the package from Grand Manan, and it was fine for a change. And we have enough for another meal.

We put up the specimens we got yesterday, this forenoon, and it did not take long. There is a beautiful bird we have collected on this mountain and so far we have not found it anywhere else. It is a highland species anyway. The back is greenish yellow, straw yellow breast with a crescent of black next to the red throat. It is one of the shrikes.

It seems too bad that we have to be here where the natives are burning the grass. What a glorious view we would have from the peak! As it is, we can't even get a picture for the smoke. We have real cold nights, and the black boys have built quite a "village" for our party. They added two more houses today. It is interesting to watch them build these structures; they begin with bamboo four or five inches through it and sixty or seventy feet long, and strip it into long slender slats. They begin by sticking an end into the ground, bending it over and down into the ground on the opposite side. When they have used the number prepared, they have a nice even cone about six feet high in the centre. Wherever the slats cross, they are tied securely. When the roofs are grassed, they gather up large bunches and these are tied together and lashed to the frame. I wondered how they were going to make the peaked top tight. It was simple enough; they picked up a huge armful of the grass and tied it firmly around the roots and turned it over so the tied end was inside. It was like a huge umbrella covering the entire top and was absolutely tight. These houses last a year when they either abandon, or burn them down. The question of housing is a simple one and only requires a few hours work. Still they are well adapted to the climate, and are as cool a shelter as one would want, to a certain extent the grass sides are porous, and the ventilation fair to good.

The chief difficulty is the white ants; in a location where the pests abound, they make short work of a house. This insect is so numerous in some places it's a real menace. Right across Africa I studied these interesting creatures. The fortress of the white ants is such a clever piece of engineering it's simply marvelous, and so well adapted to their purpose it could not be improved. In low land where conditions were favourable, I have seen ant hills twenty feet high. They are built of the materials they have at hand, the soil, bits of sand, and even bodies of dead ants. Everything is used and nothing discarded or wasted. All this material is cemented together with a secretion they manufacture from their own bodies. It makes such a valuable and hard cement the natives use it to make their cooking pots. They break down a hill, grind up the material and apply enough water to make it about the consistency of dough that is easily handled, and then mold their pots by hand. When the vessel is finished, they take a smooth stick and go over the surface until it is like glass. When it's baked in the sun it stands fire and is a serviceable article and very useful for their purposes.

The object of the "ant fortress" is to protect the throne room of the queen. I have opened a hill before now and have been surprised at the perfect network of galleries. I met a scientist who had it figured out so fine, for instance, he said a white ant such as one sees most frequently in Central Africa is approximately one-eighth of an inch high, and their fortresses are over two thousand times their own height. To equal this feat, a man would have to put up structures two and a half miles high. At the same time the hills shed the rain. I did not see it, but I have heard it on good authority, that an infuriated rhino cannot make a very definite impression on one with all its strength.

Give all my best to family and friends.

Allan L. Moses

After Allan posted his letter of July 7, he could neither send nor receive mail for a long time. During the last three weeks of July, a relatively mild yet annoying recurrence of malaria had subdued his usual good spirits and vitality. Then, too, the party made slow progress on safari (literally on foot) through equatorial Africa, far from civilization in the wilds of what was then the Belgian Congo. But another consideration also stayed his pen.

When the expedition reached Luvumba on July 22, Allan opened the medical supplies, carried half-way across Africa, for quinine. Medication and rest would speed his recovery, he knew, while "the boys" continued to take day-long treks hoping to find the prize. On July 26, four days after they had set up camp, Allan wakened from an afternoon nap and stepped out of his tent for a bit of exercise. Not far away, in a large tree, perched the elusive broadbill. Allan turned back to the tent for his small specimen gun. He arrived within shooting distance just in time to see the bird fly off but, following in the general direction of its flight, he spotted it again and collected it.

The exertion and excitement proved too much for Allan's diminished strength. When "the boys" returned to camp, they found him lying on his cot with the broadbill grasped tightly in his hand. *Pseudocalyptomena graueri* had been rediscovered! To celebrate their victory, the elated explorers treated themselves to

Pseudocalyptomena graueri.
A line drawing by A. Seidel for
*Chapin's Birds of the Belgian
Congo,* c. 1930. (AMNH)

the choicest of foods from
their limited supply.

Before the expedition, Allan
had promised that Rocke-
feller and Murphy would
make the announcement if
they succeeded in their mission, and keeping his word
meant not telling even his
family the stunning news.
The three men stayed in the
area a little while longer,
excitedly collecting several
more broadbills. Then, for
the next three months, they
made their way through the
southeastern corner of the
Congo forest, adding nearly
four hundred valuable bird
skins to their collection. Allan
resumed writing to his family.

Kita Kita, Belgian Congo
October 13, 1929

Dear folks,

Mercy knows when you will get this letter. I will send it as
soon as opportunity offers, but will continue to write whenever
I can. On this long safari, I am afraid there will not be a chance
to put it in the mail, so by the time we get to Kindu, I shall
have quite a report for you.

This has been a wonderful safari so far, and I am well. The
parts of the country we have passed through have been nothing
short of astonishing, it is like a dreamland, hard to explain and

describe. I have seen a great many of the wild animals of this continent, and I have certainly done my bit, too, in getting the birds we were sent after, the only big thing I have done for science.

I shall come home from Boma, at the mouth of the Congo [Zaire] River on the West Coast, and that should be in four or five months. I am bringing a fine elephant tusk that weighs fifty pounds. It will be a great curiosity, as I don't imagine many around home have seen one. We have collected four elephants, one with tusks weighing eighty pounds each when first removed.

I am certainly sorry I have been obliged to stay nearly two years, but the way things go here two years is nothing, it takes lots of time to do anything. The porters are so blessed slow, it is exasperating, but you can't hurry them.

Hope you got my diary of the Marungu experience. This one has been harder, as the Kandashomwa range was higher, with much more climbing to do, and very cold at over 9,000 feet near the summit. The collections in this area have been good, since it has never been thoroughly covered by naturalists before, and we have a lot of interesting specimens. I only wish you could have seen them. It is the best collection I have made, considering the quality of the individual items, including many beautiful birds, with such wonderful colours.

October 20: Our safari this morning was three hours, but tomorrow's will be longer, about four and a half. Mr. Murphy went ahead to have the elephant tusks registered, the ones we got in Kita Kita. My, it's hot here today in the middle of Africa! But it will be a great trip down the Congo River and we have been following Stanley's footsteps pretty closely. We shall be at Boma on the coast in five or six weeks, and at Coquilhatville before that, where I will surely have mail. This is all beautiful country, but I should not care to live here. This is the home of the blacks, and they are welcome to it; I never liked hot weather.

October 25: I am very tired, but in three days we will see the great river, one of the world's largest, and very soon will be back in civilization again. We have only 1,000 birds, but they are from this part of Africa, including the one we were sent for, *the very rare one,* and another that was badly needed. I think all interested will be pleased; not many expeditions get all they go for.

October 31: We left Kindu, by steamer, at the head of navigation in the Congo, at eight o'clock, Mr. Murphy and I as Mr R. had to go back to Albertville again. There was a mistake in the things we shipped from Kigoma, so the boxes are held up by customs. We will go down river to Stanleyville [Kisangani] and Mr. R. will meet us there some time next week. I will finish this letter tomorrow and mail it in Stanleyville as soon as we arrive. No mail for us at Kindu, but Mr. R. will pick up any that may be at Albertville. I hope you have sent the addresses of the English cousins, as I want to see them before I leave England.

The last trek was a hard one, eight days of straight walking, covering twenty miles in the last eight hours. But we came out of it fine. Such a beautiful forest we walked through, much of it great mahogany trees, some of them eight feet through and as straight as gun barrels. And now we are relaxing on this glorious sail down river which, by the way, at this point is not nearly as large as expected.

November 1: This is the second day on the river and now it is wide, with many villages. The natives come off in dugout canoes to meet the boat, and the passengers throw them beer bottles. We had fresh fish for dinner today, the first we have tasted since we left Lake Tanganyika five months ago.

We can get to Stanleyville from this point, one day by train and will be there a while, as we have to pack our specimens for America. The boys (Rockefeller and Murphy) may go on to Liberia on the West Coast for a few months, but I am not going with them. My contract is filled. I don't like the West Coast; my experience there in 1923 is sufficient for one lifetime.

November 17: Left Stanleyville this morning, bound for Coquilhatville [Mbandaka] where I hope to get mail. We will be in that town two weeks, then on to Boma, where we will separate for the first time since we landed on the East Coast in August, 1928. It will be a bad time to leave the tropics and start home, but it can't be helped. It appears I will have to go by way of Belgium, then over to England and on to Halifax.

Mr. R. returned yesterday from Albertville. He brought our clothes and boxes held up there in customs, so everything is now alright. While we were in Stanleyville we packed all our specimens, and the boxes are ready to ship when we reach the coastal port.

November 18: This is Sunday, and we are going downriver again. The water is very high, up to the branches of the trees and even above some of them. The weather is simply boiling from the middle of the day until midnight, but cooler towards morning. It is cloudy nearly all the time and rains every night. Have crossed the equator once and will again in a few days, on this winding trip toward the sea.

We are just now passing close by an island, and the tropical forest with its flowering trees and vines is a beautiful sight, something one will not forget very soon. The blossoms are lovely, but rarely have any perfume. There are palm trees mixed in with the other species, something we have not seen before on this cruise.

November 19: This is about four o'clock and very hot and humid. We have now stopped at a small town, where there are quite a lot of Belgians, officials of course. I see they have a tame chimpanzee that goes around to people, like a boy. They make great pets, but don't live long when tamed.

November 20: Was just on shore and took a picture of the boat. These small towns are on the bank of the river, with the natives living further inland. There is a couple of thousand white population along this part of the river, most living in brick houses, and also in Coquilhatville there is quite a large white colony.

It is great fun to see the blacks go ashore with the ship's lines. They put the spliced loop over their heads when the boat is very near the bank, then jump in the water and swim ashore. It is wire and always sinks them, but they swim with it, under water, until they get near enough to get up and walk. The vessels are so shallow they make the landing sideways against the bank, run a plank out and we simply walk ashore.

November 21: It is so calm the trees are reflected from the banks and it is lovely. On board one hears many strange tongues, Belgian, Dutch and Flemish, to name a few. I can truly say I have never seen so much beer drinking in all my life put together. These people drink all day and all night, men, women and all, no difference. About four in the afternoon they have their "afternoon tea." I will miss this when I get back as we have followed that habit ever since we started from New York.

November 23: One of the black boys jumped over just now about ten o'clock, but they put out a boat and got him. We are supposed to reach Coquilhatville today and will close this letter and send it along. If all goes well, I will be home right after you receive it, and will bring my diary with me.

Have found there is a line from Boma to the United States and if possible will come that way, otherwise, as explained will have to go to Antwerp, thence England, but I should be home in two months at the outside. I will be glad to be through with it, and to hear good old Canadian talk, and get a home-cooked meal again. In the bush one does fine, but these hotels and boats are impossible. There is a lot of food, but the way the cooks spoil it is a sin and a shame.

When we got to Kindu, at the end of our last safari, I was a fair looking specimen, but two weeks at a hotel and the trip on the boats down river and I am rattling around in my clothes. I am still able to digest an assortment of leather, "food" that comes to the table looking like nothing I have ever seen; from the odour it is something that passed away in another age; some prehistoric animal of which nothing is preserved but the smell, and that reaches to high heaven! I hide as much away as I can and throw it overboard; in that way I have disposed of enough to save one life anyway.

Arrived here in Coquilhatville at one o'clock and this letter will go along with the steamer. I hope to get mail here. Like Stanleyville, this is a very pretty town. The river bank is a little high and the town shows up well, but the equator runs through it. See you soon!

Allan L. Moses

When the specimens Allan and his two friends had collected in Africa all arrived safely in New York, Dr. J.P. Chapin, the curator of African birds at the American Museum of Natural History, personally checked each item with great satisfaction. He was writing his lengthy *Birds of the Belgian Congo* and, because of the rare contents of the crates and cartons, he was able to extend the species list considerably and add new information about species that had been inadequately described. In his introduction to the first volume of his work, he said:

> Marungu, the highland region southwest of Lake Tanganyika, was one of the districts I wished to see investigated. So in 1928, when my friends Messrs. J. Sterling Rockefeller and Charles G.B. Murphy expressed a desire to make a collecting trip to Africa, I urged them to go to Marungu. They secured the services of Allan L. Moses as taxidermist, and started from Dar-es-Salaam on the East African coast. After visiting Albertville they reached Moba on February 19, 1929, and travelled southward over the highlands to Lake

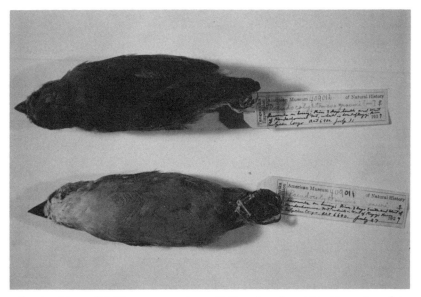

Study skins of African green broadbills, the tiny (4³/₄"), colourful flycatchers rediscovered by the Rockefeller-Murphy-Moses expedition of 1928-29. (AMNH)

Suse and the Kampemba River, close to the Rhodesian border. Then from Seleme they traversed the highlands again by a more westerly route, and returned to Moba on May 18. About 600 birds were collected during the survey of Marungu, among them several species never before observed in Congo territory. Messrs. Rockefeller, Murphy, and Moses turned next to the Ruzizi Valley and the mountains to the west, and there made an earnest and successful search for the green broadbill, *Pseudocalyptomena*. Finally they travelled through the southeastern corner of the Congo forest to Itula and Kindu, and down the Congo River to its mouth. Between Ruzizi and Kindu an additional collection of 385 bird-skins was obtained.

Fulfilling their agreement with Allan to make their great discovery known to the scientific community, Rockefeller and

Murphy wrote a six-page report, "The Rediscovery of *Pseudo-calyptomena*," which came out in *The Auk* in January 1932. After recounting the history of the scientific knowledge of the bird, they described it in detail and explained the origin of its name:

> The broadbills are a family of small birds outwardly resembling Old World flycatchers and with similar broad beaks, but plainly differentiated in their outer primary quills, the scales of their feet, and their syrinx or voice-organ with far simpler musculature. Less than two decades ago it was believed that the broadbills lived only in the Oriental Region, from Southern Asia to Borneo, Sumatra, and the Philippines. Lord Rothschild noted a certain resemblance between the new bird from the mountains of the Kivu district and *Calyptomena*, a green broadbill of Borneo and the Malay Peninsula, but did not think it denoted true relationship.

Rothschild called the bird *Pseudocalyptomena*, indicating a superficial resemblance to the oriental broadbills, an approach scientists sometimes take in naming species not definitely identified. Rothschild added the Latinized name of the Austrian scientist who brought that first specimen to Europe, calling his specimen *Pseudocalyptomena graueri*. Building on Rothschild's description, Rockefeller and Murphy reported the following:

> [In] colour, their "Pseudo" is mostly of a bright grass-green, its pattern is varied with pale blue on throat and chest, ear-coverts, and beneath the tail; the forehead is greenish buff streaked with brown; and the cheeks are spotted with blackish.

After reviewing the long search — described by Allan in detail in his journals and summarized by Dr. Chapin in *Birds of the Belgian Congo* — Rockefeller and Murphy revealed to the world how the precious specimen had been collected:

> We reached Luvumba on July 22, 1929. Would Fortune favour us here? It took four days to answer the question affirmatively. Then in the upper end of the valley, a gun-shot from the stream, Moses secured our first "Pseudo" — the second known specimen, which proved to be an adult male. With what satisfaction we measured it, noted the colour of its iris, bill and feet . . . During the next two weeks a half-dozen additional specimens were secured about Luvumba. Two of them were preserved in alcohol . . . One of our spirit specimens was later submitted to Dr. P.R. Lowe of the British Museum for anatomical study.

So it was confirmed: the rarity was a true broadbill, although the "psuedo" stayed in its name to distinguish it from all the other broadbills. Rockefeller and Murphy underlined the importance of the discovery to the world of ornithology and to the success of the expedition:

> Many "rare" birds of the tropics have little save scarcity to commend them. Others possess beauty as well. But this green broadbill, in addition to being rare and beautiful, merited the attention of the anatomist as well as the student of bird distribution. It was indeed an object of envy among naturalists.

There is good reason for the careful, even sometimes cautious, presentation of new information, but the collection of that first *Pseudocalyptomena graueri* on July 26, 1929, and the events that followed, justify the enthusiasm that Rockefeller and Murphy could not conceal even in a scientific article.

SEVEN

The New Adventure: Grand Manan

ALLAN LEFT WEST AFRICA at the end of November 1929, and finally got home to Grand Manan early in January 1930. After living in the tropics for so long, he found winter weather a violent surprise. But the Island temperatures were so much milder than those he had suffered while crossing the Atlantic that winter on Grand Manan seemed warm and peaceful in comparison. Family and friends joyfully welcomed him into their midst again. They had all read Sarah's accounts of his adventures in the local papers, and everywhere he went they greeted him exuberantly. Pleased as he was with such a reception, and content as he was to be home again, he longed to tell his friends and relatives about finding the African green broadbill, but he had been sworn to secrecy by Rockefeller and Murphy. He had also been sworn to secrecy about a great plan he and Rockefeller had made.

Although the explorers had celebrated Allan's shooting of the *Pseudocalyptomena graueri* near Luvumba, in the Lusigi River Valley, 6,600 feet above sea level, Allan's bargaining that day ensured that the benefits of the victory reached far beyond the Congo and the American Museum of Natural History. Happy as he had been to catch the African bird, he had had other birds in a far different setting on his mind. Seated around the campfire that evening of July 26, 1929, the three colleagues had replayed the day's events in great detail again and again, made their notes, and speculated about what it could mean. Sterling Rockefeller felt particular gratitude, and he told Allan he would like to mark the achievement in some special way. Allan needed no further prompting. "For a fraction of what this expedition has cost," he told his friend, "you could buy a group of three islands in the Grand Manan area, have them declared a sanctuary, and thus save the Bay of Fundy eider ducks." The three explorers enthusiastically turned this idea over many times until, exhausted but jubilant, they retired to their tents for the night. Over the next few days, they examined every detail of Allan's proposal until they reached an agreement. Rockefeller would buy the Three Islands group off Grand Manan if the owners could be persuaded to sell; Allan would become head of the project, and he would serve as one of the wardens for the sanctuary. The plan was based on the premise that the few surviving nesting pairs of eiders would multiply if they were protected. If this premise could be tested and proven true, one of the most important breeding grounds on the Bay of Fundy would be saved.

For the time being, Allan had to keep his secrets. Revealing the first would be a breach of his contract as well as his faith with his friends, and revealing the second would certainly increase the price of the land. He must simply wait patiently until Rockefeller and Murphy's report could be published, and work discreetly towards the Three Island goal as circumstances permitted.

He had much to do. In February he received a letter from Dr. F.H. Kennard of the Museum of Comparative Zoology at Harvard University. "You see your fame has, more or less, spread abroad throughout the land," Kennard said, "and I had heard that you were back from your African trip." Would Allan supply the museum with some specimens — double-crested cormorants, murres, a Kumlien's gull, a razorbill, and a few purple sandpipers in breeding plumage? This assignment took Allan several months to complete, partly of course because the birds did not all appear on Grand Manan at the same time, but partly because he ran into almost as much difficulty with the U.S. Customs Office as he did in choosing suitable days for collecting specimens. Finally, in May, Kennard wrote, "We've got that Eastport fellow so he eats out of my hand. Just sends me a paper to sign, swearing to God that the birds are for scientific purposes and not to wear on my wife's hat, and then the birds come right along."

In the meantime, quietly pursuing his plan for the Three Islands, Allan held a confidential discussion with Ralph Beal of North Head, a tax collector, long-time local school board officer and Justice of the Peace. Beal agreed at once to act as agent in attempting to buy the Three Islands group for Rockefeller, but he would take title in his own name. Even if millions of dollars worth of assets lay behind the actual buyer, the final deal would still depend on getting the right price. So they waited. On April 5, Rockefeller sent a telegram from Greenwich, Connecticut, authorizing Allan to close deals with the two separate owners of the islands, according to agreed limits and conditions. He also consented to take Ralph Griffin onto the payroll as the second warden, but they must "continue withholding information as to buyer."

Beal had been able to get a commitment for the sale of Kent Island from McLaughlin Brothers Ltd., a Seal Cove firm. Kent was the largest of the three islands, with an area of approximately 150 acres. The other two islands, Hay with thirty acres, and Sheep with twenty acres, were owned by Henry Ingalls. He had lived on Hay Island for many years, and his fish sheds were there, too. Though they negotiated intermittently for several months, he refused to sell even when Rockefeller — through Beal — offered him life tenancy. Henry Ingalls loved the isolated spot. Wreathed in fog for two or three months of the year, it was an idyllic place where myriad birds of many species filled the air with their calls and songs. Lobster, ground fish and herring lurked in their turn hardly more than a dory's length from shore. There was garden space and enough pasture to keep a milk cow and raise young beef for winter. Supplemented by driftwood, Hay Island's spruce and fir, though stunted by salty storms, provided ample fuel for Fundy winters. Even had Henry Ingalls known that it was a Rockefeller who wanted to buy his islands, and that he would offer a good part of the family's worldly goods for them, he would still have refused to give up title to his domain. Today, Hay and Sheep Islands are owned by Owen Ingalls Jr. and Jack Ingalls.

Understandably, their failure to acquire Hay and Sheep Islands greatly disappointed the project planners. However, they achieved a compromise: a contract of easement gave sanctuary staff access to the two smaller islands for "scientific purposes." That would permit making bird population counts, keeping nesting records, and carrying out related studies. On his part, Henry Ingalls reserved the right to shoot ducks on his own property, in season, considering them part of his food supply and hunting one of the few recreations his island provided.

In spite of this setback, however, creating the sanctuary continued apace. Ralph Beal bought Kent Island for about $25,000 and transferred title to Rockefeller on July 14, 1930. Ottawa approved the use of the island as a protected sanctuary (actually a private refuge), and the organizers began to advertise it as such. The two wardens moved to Kent Island early in June 1930, to set up headquarters and living space in an old house that, along with a barn, a herring smokehouse, two sheds and a camp, were included in the sale of the island. The wardens also took charge of the cow and the flock of sheep that came with the land. Rockefeller paid Allan and Ralph Griffin each $1,000 a year. While that may seem a paltry sum today, it was generous for the time.

And so began the challenging task. It now seems remarkable that, under the circumstances, the project got under way at all. While Allan and his colleagues were still trekking through the Congo forest, the stock market crash of October 24, 1929, had brought many of the Wall Street empires tumbling to the ground. The crash had followed a series of financial crises in Europe, and suddenly most of the world was plunged into a depression. Many erstwhile millionaires became penniless overnight. Eventually, the U.S. government had to declare a "bank holiday" until order and an element of trust could be restored. Factories and business places closed and millions were jobless. The "hungry thirties" had begun.

Because of its immensity and diversity, the Rockefeller wealth apparently did not dwindle as seriously as many other private fortunes did. Much of it had come from the giant Standard Oil Company which, in 1882, was valued at more than $70 million, and that in the next half century doubled its worth several times. Even the 1892 court order that broke Standard Oil into twenty separate companies, so it could no longer hold a monopoly, failed to halt its growth. Thus, even after the crash, Sterling Rockefeller could still afford to buy Kent Island and operate it as a private bird sanctuary.

With their home gardens, the cattle they raised for beef and milk, the clams available for the digging, and abundant fish of many kinds, the residents of Grand Manan suffered far less during the Depression than city dwellers did. But cash was a rare commodity. Labourers received $1 a day when work was available, the same as junior bank clerks. Teachers worked for $300 to $500 a year. A good catch of ground fish sometimes brought less than the cost of the fisherman's gasoline, and smoked herring dropped as low as fifteen cents for an eighteen-pound box, if they could be sold at all. Only a few senior federal civil servants had salaries approaching the $1,000 a year that Rockefeller paid his Kent Island wardens.

Nevertheless, Rockefeller expected Allan and Ralph Griffin to run a very tight ship. He wanted them to generate as much revenue as possible, with a view to making the project nearly self-sustaining. He overlooked nothing. One of the chattels that came with the property was a salted horse hide, worth a few dollars for leather; messages had to be exchanged about its disposal, since the nearest tannery was on the mainland. The flock of sheep had to be culled, and plans were made to bring in new rams to strengthen the bloodline. Silver foxes were purchased to start a small fur ranch, a venture that disturbed Allan because one or two escapees could destroy the very purpose of the sanctuary. Ingalls Head, the nearest village on the main island of Grand Manan, is about five miles due north of Kent Island, and by early fall Rockefeller had bought the wardens a new Cape Island motor boat so they could pick up supplies and mail at convenient times. But, he warned Allan, "Don't drive it too fast

Robie W. Tufts
(1884-1982). (W. Earl Godfrey)

at first. The engine will last twice as long." For a time, it appeared to Allan and Ralph that they might have to add weir-tending to their list of duties. When McLaughlin Brothers sold Kent Island, they reserved ownership of shares in the Bar Herring Weir, and Rockefeller decided he should buy those interests as well. Fortunately for Allan and Ralph, nothing came of the proposal. With all their extra chores, plus cultivating a large garden from which they were expected to "get good money," they worked long hours, particularly in that first year.

Sterling Rockefeller paid a visit to his Bay of Fundy island in late summer, the first of several inspection trips. Between ongoing plans for the sanctuary and their experiences in Africa, he and Allan had much to talk about. They remained good friends in spite of several differences of opinion. Rockefeller's decision to call the place "Kent Island Farm" was not well received at all. Allan went along with it, because of his respect for "Rocky," as he called him, and for the ultimate importance the conservation program would have for the ecology of the Bay of Fundy. But the local people never used the name, it seems never to have appeared in the press, and eventually it passed out of memory.

An early visitor to the sanctuary was one of the few people who had known from the very beginning who was behind the scheme — Robie W. Tufts of Wolfville, N.S., Chief Migratory Bird Officer for the Maritime Provinces. A long-standing friend and frequent guest of the Moses family, he was pleased with the work that Allan was doing at Kent Island and the long-term benefits it would have for the entire Bay of Fundy. He had

strongly recommended the
sanctuary plan to the federal
government. From his ap-
pointment in 1919 until
1932, Tufts was "the long
arm of the law" around
coastal regions of the Mari-
times. During that period, it
was illegal to pick gulls'
eggs, and news of his arrival
on Grand Manan would flash
through the villages in no
time. "Tufts is here! Pass it
on." How he managed to be
in so many places — at nesting time in the spring and at
hunting time in the fall —
was always a mystery. With
his several full-time assis-

Nesting eider, alert to the threat
of intruders. (BC)

tants, his honorary officers, and his seasonal wardens, Tufts established a healthy respect for the "bird laws." Though he may
not have appeared so to offenders, he was a kind man who made
many friends wherever his duties took him. In 1932, the Royal
Canadian Mounted Police took over the enforcement of the Migratory Birds Act and so relieved Tufts of that part of his
mandate. He concentrated on public relations and conservation
education until he retired in 1947, and from then until his death
in 1982, his great zest for nature and the outdoors continued to
fuel his research and writing. In all, this great conservation pio-
neer had over sixty articles, essays and books on birds to his
credit.

In the spring of 1931, the crucial first nesting season of the
new regime began. Each year, as the eider breeding season ap-
proaches, one of the many dramas of the natural world begins to
unfold as if adhering to a master script. About the end of
March, common eiders from northern Canada that have been
wintering and feeding around the Three Islands group gather in

Eider incubating her eggs in a canopied nest on Kent Island. (BC)

great flocks and head for their nesting grounds closer to the subarctic. Then, during the first two weeks of April, eiders wintering in more southerly climes move into the area and start feeding on small shellfish on the shoal grounds around the islands. Soon, their courtship begins. By early May, they start to nest, and then the male leaves all the rest of the effort to his mate. Allan and Ralph watched as more and more of their substantial nests, lined with enough down to cover the eggs and keep them warm when the mothers needed a break, appeared on the island. Most females laid four eggs, and then they incubated them for twenty-eight days. Almost as soon as the yellow ducklings came out of their shells, the mothers took them for their first swim. Unfortunately, female eiders are much too trusting of their fellow creatures. Some set up housekeeping in ill-concealed places, and others hatched their babies quite a distance from shore. Unfriendly eyes watched that first walk to the sea, a journey more hazardous for being longer. Nevertheless, Allan and Ralph did all they could to provide the nesting birds and their young with protection from their natural predators. Their human predators had ceased egg picking, of course, because of the sanctuary, and hunting was outlawed too. The success of the

1931 breeding season hastened the re-establishment of the eider flocks.

Allan and Ralph recorded the highlights of it all and, as well as performing their regular duties, they prepared detailed reports to Sterling Rockefeller. He wanted "to be kept informed of everything" that happened, and they made every effort to do just that. Allan took their reports home for Sarah to edit and type. For two friends well attuned to nature, the overall assignment seemed an ideal way to earn a living. It was all much to their liking except for writing the reports — they would much rather be out banding birds and learning about flight patterns. Yet they never lost sight of the larger purpose of the owner's interests, simply because it matched their own long-term hopes. Further, tangible results constantly rewarded their efforts as the entire Three Islands ecosystem responded dramatically to the organized programme of conservation.

Planning for the Long Term

Dr. Alfred O. Gross, professor of biology at Bowdoin College in Brunswick, Maine, had been keenly interested in the Kent Island project since first hearing of it. Sterling Rockefeller readily gave Dr. Gross permission to go to the island in the spring of 1932 to study the eider ducks. His research there and his conversations with Allan sowed the seeds of an idea. He had long wished that Bowdoin had a natural study area. This concept was relatively new in academic circles. Like the biology departments in most academic institutions, Gross's department still depended upon relatively brief field trips to supplement the textbooks. While Bowdoin did have a tradition of unhurried summer field trips to Labrador and elsewhere, such long-distance excursions were too costly and exclusive to be part of the permanent program. Yet, to become competent in new natural science disciplines such as wildlife management, marine biology and ornithology, students needed longer and more intense experience in the real world. On rare occasions, fortunate students man-

Dr. Alfred O. Gross
(1883-1970). (BC)

aged to find places on carefully staffed museum expeditions or privately sponsored excursions of various kinds, and Commander Donald Baxter MacMillan, a famous Arctic explorer and Bowdoin alumnus, reserved places for several students on his northern voyages each year. But these few opportunities did not solve the general problem.

Dr. Gross thought that Kent Island would make an ideal natural study area for Bowdoin College. And the time for Bowdoin grew more opportune with each passing day. As the Depression worsened, Sterling Rockefeller was understandably more preoccupied with matters nearer home in Connecticut and New York than he was with the operation of the tiny island sanctuary in the Bay of Fundy. Yet he did not want to sacrifice the good work he had already accomplished at Kent Island by honouring his agreement with Allan Moses. He believed that Kent Island held great potential, not only for continuing conservation of birdlife, but also for learning more about the natural sciences. It was not in the tradition of the Rockefeller family to make decisions with long-term consequences before investigating thoroughly. As soon as spring weather permitted in 1934, Rockefeller invited a group of New England ornithologists aboard his yacht for a sail to the Three Islands. There, he asked their advice on how best to carry out his twin objectives of conservation and research. From this consultation stemmed the decision that, once details could be worked out to suit both parties, he would give Kent Island to Bowdoin College for use as an "outdoor laboratory," if the sanctuary would be maintained.

Bowdoin, for its part, set about to investigate the benefits of

Bowdoin students in the 1934 vanguard at Kent Island. (GMM)

the plan at first hand. In May 1934, when Commander MacMillan left Boothbay Harbor, Maine, for another expedition in his specially built schooner *Bowdoin*, he had aboard a survey party sent out to examine the feasibility of the Three Islands group as a natural study area. He dropped off four students, with their supplies, on Kent Island: W.A.O. (Bill) Gross (the professor's son), Burt Whitman, Jr., Paul Favour, Jr., and Frederick A. Fisher. The young men camped there, and Allan and Ralph Griffin helped them as much as they could. They put the sanctuary boat at their disposal so they could examine the outer ledge tops and nearby islands, and they showed them the records they had kept since 1930. The students became enthusiastic about the proposal — as Bill Gross wrote later, "We revelled in the great bird rookeries, in the teeming life of the lagoons offshore, in the beauty of the region, and in our discovery of a land the naturalist had apparently overlooked." Allan and Ralph, too, rejoiced at the possibilities that a permanent arrangement with Bowdoin might bring to realization.

Three months later, Commander MacMillan picked the students up again on his way back from the Arctic. In their report, Bill Gross and his colleagues strongly recommended that Kent Island become an off-campus research area and, with this endorsement, the board of governors "gladly accepted" Rockefeller's proposal and appointed Dr. Alfred Gross director. The title deed contained very clear conditions. Bowdoin would use Kent Island "for scientific purposes only," maintain the bird sanctuary, and employ a "watchman" there from May 15 to September 1 each year. Failure to honour those specifics would mean that ownership would revert to the Rockefeller family. Although the deed did not pass to Bowdoin until January 9, 1936, Dr. Gross organized the first Bowdoin expedition to Kent Island for the spring and summer of 1935.

Allan Moses and Ralph Griffin retired from the scene and returned permanently to their homes in North Head. Allan's family life had taken some unhappy turns since the Kent Island sanctuary was established. Early in 1931, he realized that Sarah had not been in her usual good health for some time, but she seemed to respond to new medication. Thus, to him particularly, her death on December 17, at age fifty-four, was a shock indeed. She had been a capable catalyst in the family, mothering her three daughters, making a home for her aging father and Allan, managing their correspondence and, in addition, carrying on her own gardening and writing. Allan could scarcely imagine what his life would be like without her presence.

The most immediate problems centred on John Russell, then seventy-eight years old. He had become a legend in his own time. He was still active and very much in charge of the fish plant, but the past year had brought a considerable difference in his mental and physical condition. It would not be long before his drive to carry on would be diminished. His own awareness of this fact only hastened his infirmity. Another difficulty was connected with the depressed economy. The market for fish products had almost disappeared. Exporters around the Bay of Fundy, eager to sell, were in desperate straits and hastened their own ruin by underbidding. At times, dried salt cod and hake brought only two or three cents a pound, hardly enough to pay for the salt. The market still existed, primarily in the West Indies and southern United States, but consumers there had no money. Canada had fish, beef, potatoes and wheat in abundance, but these products could not be distributed fairly, even within the country, and very little got to the export markets. Grand Manan residents took the matter into their own hands in a minor way by carrying cured fish to the Annapolis Valley in Nova Scotia and trading it for apples and other such "luxury" items.

Fortunately, the Moses family had ample resources to tide them over for a fairly long period. Much of the profit from the business had been saved to purchase bank stock, then perhaps the most secure commercial investment. While a great many banks failed in the United States during the Depression, the strong Canadian system, founded on Scottish principles and branch banking, rode out the troubled times. Nevertheless, throughout the 1930s people worried that the banks could fail here as well, and in that case the family savings could disappear. John Russell Moses never fully recovered from the double blow of this economic disruption and Sarah's death.

Two of Allan's nieces lived in Bermuda. Florence had gone there on a visit, decided to make it her home and, in 1930, she had married Ralph Swift. Full of the family's spirit of adventure, Florence and her new husband had crossed from Bermuda to New York City in a fifteen-foot sailboat. Sarah confided to a friend that the 800-mile voyage, which took her daughter and son-in-law seventeen days, "nearly finished me." Mary, Sarah's youngest, was spending two years in Bermuda attending finishing school when Sarah died, and therefore Helen, who was still on Grand Manan, took over the management of the household temporarily. After a time, she and her husband, Fred Frye, an officer on the Grand Manan Ferry, moved to the mainland to make their own way in life. Mary returned to Canada, and in 1933 she married Raymond Wilson of Digdeguash. The Depression took its toll on Raymond's weir fishing business, so Mary and Raymond took over managing the Moses home for awhile. This allowed Allan to concentrate his attention on the operation of the Kent Island sanctuary, and Raymond carried out security patrols there from time to time, too.

When Kent Island passed into the hands of Bowdoin College, it seemed only fitting that Ernest Joy, who had discovered the albatross off Machias Seal Island over twenty years before, should become the new resident naturalist and warden. Fifty-eight years of age, he had accumulated many years of sea time as a fisherman and former member of the Canadian Life Saving Service. This experience, together with his unusually wide knowledge of birdlife, made him an invaluable contributor to the new Scientific Station. Outer Wood Island, his old haunt during his days with the Life Saving Service, had large colonies of Leach's storm-petrels and herring gulls, and lesser numbers of other species. Flocks of sheep lived there, along with thousands of domestic rabbits that had gone wild and inbred until their coats presented every colour in the rabbit spectrum. These rabbits competed with the petrels for burrowing space in the spongy soil. Wreathed in fog for much of the summer season, Outer Wood Island was a place of mystery and magic for Ernest Joy's young Bowdoin explorers. Bowdoin College agreed to pay Ernest $300 per year. The house on Kent Island was thrown in, and Ernest supplemented his income by trapping muskrats, which one year brought in an extra $545.

Allan's bold suggestion, made that evening in the middle of Africa, had become a reality. In the five years during which he and Ralph Griffin had acted as Rockefeller's wardens, he had seen the number of nesting eiders grow from "several" to several hundred. His conservation objective had proven not merely realistic, but successful far beyond his original dream. Not only that, but Kent Island now had a future more secure than he had ever dared to expect.

EIGHT

Home from the Hills and the Sea

Here he lies where he longed to be;
Home is the sailor, home from the sea
And the hunter home from the hill.

— Robert Louis Stevenson, "Requiem"

*A*FTER SPENDING SO much time off-island, Allan was happy to take part in community life again. He became active in the local Oddfellows Lodge and took up many of his former pursuits, such as hunting and professional collecting. In that period, too, he became one of the founders of the Grand Manan Branch of the New Brunswick Fish and Game Protective Association, and he contributed a great deal of time to its projects. When they discovered that prime trout were escaping from Eel Lake via the brook that emptied over the high cliffs at Ashburton Head, he and other members installed a screen to hold them back. He helped mainland professionals do plankton and temperature tests in all of the Island lakes and ponds. With this information, the Branch knew where to plant new fish fry. They reintroduced trout into several bodies of water, land-locked salmon into one, and bass into another.

Restocking the Island with moose was considered, but when the organizers saw that the experiment had little chance of success, they abandoned the idea. They did bring in white-tailed deer stock to rejuvenate the local herds, but one shipment proved to be more of a nuisance than a benefit. Two of the three animals were orphans that had been reared in pens by a mainland warden and, since they arrived in Grand Manan the day before hunting season opened, they had to stay in pens for another month. Three times the spoiled deer were liberated into the wilds of the Island, the last time carried by horse-drawn wagon about ten miles into the woods. Locked out of their familiar pen, hungering for the vegetables they were accustomed to, they became notorious garden foragers. All met early deaths, one by shooting and two in car accidents. They painfully reminded Island conservationists that wildlife can never be truly "managed."

Nearly all the Fish and Game Protective Association ventures proved successful, except the introduction of ring-necked pheasants. Eggs were brought in from the mainland and hatched under domestic hens, and the chicks were liberated as soon as they were large enough to fend for themselves. For a time the beautiful birds seemed to flourish, but it eventually became apparent that they could not adapt to Island life. Most agreed that the lack of sufficient food seeds doomed the pheasant project. Allan, however, had a different opinion. While agreeing that the scarcity of suitable food was a factor, he suspected that feral domestic cats were to blame. While he liked cats where they belonged, he knew from experience that once they began living in the wild they became highly successful predators of young birds. He detested stray cats with a vengeance, as he did crows, who got on his "unwanted" list because of their partiality to the eggs of song birds. He did not even allow crows in the Moses bird collection.

In spite of small setbacks, the association did a great deal of good. The government finally yielded to local pressure and appointed two full-time game wardens instead of relying on seasonal officers. Allan's old friend Ralph Griffin, who had worked with him when Sterling Rockefeller owned Kent Island, was one of the new wardens.

However interesting he found his fish and game activities, Allan soon found he was needed at home more and more. John Russell's illness had taken a serious turn, and the care of the ageing patriarch, even with the help of a practical nurse, became a demanding task. That was long before the Island had a nursing home, and four years before the local hospital opened. Home care for the ill and elderly was all that was available, and fortunately the capable local doctor, John F. Macaulay, still made house calls. On February 27, 1936, John Russell Moses died at the age of eighty-three.

For a time, local men operated the fish plant that John Russell had built and managed so successfully, but soon Allan sold the business. Very shortly, the buildings fell silent, and they have now crumbled and disappeared from the North Head scene. Allan's patrimony had decreased during the Depression years, but he still had enough money to keep him in comfortable circumstances for the rest of his life. The security provided by John Russell's careful financial management had enabled Allan to do many beneficial things that otherwise he could not have afforded to do. Allan was no spendthrift; far from it. But, thanks to his father's business acumen, he had been free to do the things that interested him the most, out in the world of nature.

Much to the surprise of even his closest friends, Allan became a Benedick after having enjoyed bachelorhood for fifty-five years. On March 26, 1936, he married Mabel Claire (Guptill) Kent, a widow who lived nearby and who, with her late husband Manuel, had owned the historic Marathon Hotel. Once again there was a family atmosphere in the Moses home. As in most successful marriages, the couple had to make compromises. Allan had to give up some of the freedom that no doubt had kept him single for so long, in exchange for the amenities of a domestic life. Yet time had decreased the boundless energy that had served him so well, and now he was more inclined to talk about roaming the shores and fields, or about his great feat of walking through equatorial Africa. On her part, Mabel had to accommodate to the personal forces that motivate a naturalist and get to know the frequent visitors from near and far who came to talk endlessly of birds and animals. However, she put her own background in operating a hotel to good use, and she was a gracious hostess.

Compromise aside, the two found mutual comfort in the marriage. They travelled to places of special interest and entertained their friends. They bought a car — Allan's first — and, though he chose not to learn to drive, younger relatives took them on weekend jaunts.

Allan began to get involved in the civic life of Grand Manan. When the hospital was established in 1940, he became a member of the first board of directors. The several local school districts had been consolidated in 1943 to provide a larger tax base, and secondary level courses had been offered in temporary quarters since that time. Post-war prosperity made it possible to build the Island's first high school, at Grand Harbour, and Grand Manan High School opened in September 1948. Allan observed this outburst of activity with the sense of pride shared by so many. Yet it seemed that, even as the community was taking on new life, his own time was running out. Nearing seventy, he was concerned about the fate of the family museum. The National Museum of Natural Sciences in Ottawa had made overtures, but he didn't encourage them, although he left open the possibility of later discussions.

Madawaska Construction Ltd., of Edmundston, won the high school building contract, and Dr. P.C. LaPorte, the president of the company, visited Grand Manan. Fletcher W. Harvey, chairman of the interim school board, took over the pleasant task of showing the visitor around. This tour, like most, included the Moses Museum in North Head. Dr. LaPorte was amazed. When he found out that Ottawa wanted to acquire the collection, he argued that this Grand Manan and Bay of Fundy treasure should never leave the Island. Of course, Allan agreed. The community also recognized the value of the Moses collection and wanted to keep it at home, yet they seemed to need a catalyst before they could act. The man from Edmundston successfully carried out that role. The school board liked the idea of having custody of such realistic natural science teaching aids, but they could not impose a supplementary budget for the purchase of the impressive array of specimens. The Board of Trade responded to Fletcher Harvey's appeal and agreed to carry out a fundraising campaign, if necessary, and in the meantime to assist in other ways.

On March 22, 1951, a Board of Trade committee, headed by Fletcher Harvey and including Howard T. Douglasss, supervising principal of the school district, met to negotiate with Allan. When they asked him how much he might want for the Moses collection, Allan replied that it was a part of Grand Manan and must not be sent away. He had been thinking about making some kind of transfer ever since the high school had been completed. It was now his wish to present the collection to the community of Grand Manan at no cost whatever. On that dramatic note, planning began at once.

A vacant room in the basement of the high school was made available to house and display the gift. Volunteer carpenters helped Charles Titus, the school custodian, to rebuild the display cases, and in August, Allan's specimens were moved by school bus to their new location. The Moses Memorial Museum of Natural History was officially opened on October 17, 1951. At the ceremony, Allan passed a title document, in trust for the community, to Elmer N. Wilcox, then chairman of the school board. Dr. W. Austin Squires, head of the department of natural science at the New Brunswick Museum in Saint John, gave the address. He said, "For several years I have been collecting information about the New Brunswick birds, and have been particularly interested in locating specimens in the great museums. You will be interested to know that I have come across specimens collected by Mr. Moses again and again — in the National Museums of Canada, in the Chicago Natural History Museum, in the Museum of Comparative Zoology at Harvard University, in the American Museum of Natural History, New York, and in the great collection of the Royal Ontario Museum of Zoology in Toronto." Turning to Grand Manan's place in the story of North American bird life, he remarked, "Since 1850 nearly every well-known ornithologist of the United States and Canada and many less well-known have visited these islands at one time or another. It would appear to me that ornithologists have visited these islands about ten times as often as the rest of New Brunswick."

In stressing the need for conservation, Dr. Squires reviewed the sorry history of humans and birds, and recounted the species now vanished from the earth. Yet there were records of success, as well:

> The story of the eider duck is different and credit must be given to Allan Moses. In the 1920s this magnificent duck had almost vanished as a breeding bird in the Bay of Fundy when Mr. Moses interested J.S. Rockefeller in their plight. Rockefeller bought Kent Island, the chief breeding place of the eider, and made it a sanctuary. Later the island was given to Bowdoin College and a research station was set up there. The eider has made an amazing comeback, thus demonstrating the importance of protection in preserving our wildlife.

While many in the audience already knew the essentials of the address, it was important to hear these things from a person of Dr. Squires's stature.

Dr. LaPorte, by that time president of the newly organized Canadian Woodcarvers' Association, had carved a beautiful plaque to be placed at the door of the Memorial Museum. He presented it to Eric V. Horsman, the new supervising principal, who carried it downstairs to the museum room and installed it. To be recognized and honoured by so many in his own community gave Allan great pleasure, and this presentation programme was one of the most heart-warming events of his life.

Though the responsibility of caring for the Moses collection had been transferred along with the gift, Allan continued to help out, making labels and instructing the new custodians. He also added several more specimens, the last one a clapper rail which, like so many others in the collection, was the first collected in New Brunswick. This rare visitor, obviously in trouble, had been discovered in January 1952, at Castalia Marsh by Theodore Green, then president of the local Fish and Game Branch. It was in a weakened condition, due no doubt to recent storms in this strange northern clime, and by the time a bird dog re-

Allan and L.K. Ingersoll examine bank swallow nests
at Red Point, Grand Manan Island, during the filming of
"The Bird Man of Grand Manan," July 1952. (NFB)

trieved it, it was dead. Allan identified it and mounted it for the
high school collection. As it turned out, it was his final contribution.

Late in June 1952, a camera crew from the National Film
Board arrived on Grand Manan to film a sketch of the Allan
Moses story. The Odeon chain of theatres would distribute it as
part of the "Eye Witness" monthly newsmagazine series popular
in Canada at that time. Tom Farley directed the project, called
"The Bird Man of Grand Manan." The filming was a novel experience for Allan and the friends who participated as extras, and
they all had fun. The story was based at the high school, but an
important sequence was shot at Machias Seal Island. On a sunny
July day, stars and extras, crew and boatmen ate their picnic
lunch with flocks of terns and puffins protesting overhead. Just
offshore, they could see the South East Breaker where, nearly

forty years earlier, an albatross had wandered into the history of the Island and of North American ornithology.

Nearly a year later, Knight's Theatre at Grand Harbour was packed for the world premiere of the little movie before it was shown across the continent and in Great Britain. But "The Bird Man of Grand Manan" became a final salute to an outstanding citizen. Three weeks before the premiere, Allan was admitted to the local hospital, and on March 23, 1953, he died at the age of seventy-two. At the Church of the Ascension, the Rev. A.A.T. Northrup, rector of the Anglican Parish of Grand Manan, concluded his remarks at the funeral by quoting Longfellow:

> Lives of great men oft remind us
> We can make our lives sublime,
> And, departing, leave behind us
> Footprints on the sands of time.

To Allan's widow, the family and the many friends, it seemed a fitting epitaph to the memory of Allan Leopold Moses.

NINE

The Legacies of Allan Moses

The Bowdoin College Scientific Station

OVER HALF A CENTURY has passed since Bowdoin College established its Scientific Station on Kent Island. In that time, the place has reverted as nearly as possible to its ancient purpose as the focal point of a thriving ecosystem, nurtured yet undisturbed by the young Bowdoin naturalists and their mentors. After the island passed into Bowdoin's hands, Allan Moses had little direct influence on its affairs, but his contribution has never been forgotten.

Bowdoin's new outdoor laboratory took its name from its first owner, John Kent, who arrived there from England in 1798. He made a comfortable if somewhat restricted living from the land and the sea, and he sometimes worked as a Bay of Fundy pilot. When he died, his widow Susannah remained on the island alone. One night, a brigantine of British registry was sailing up the Bay in thick fog. The captain, well-fortified with Jamaican rum, took the wheel as the vessel neared the dangerous Murre Ledges. In his overloaded condition, he saw a witch who offered to guide the brig safely through the reefs. Following her, he smashed the vessel on the rocks. The officers and crew escaped to Kent Island in the lifeboats. They took shelter in Susannah's home, but the captain — no doubt still suffering from the rum — swore she was the witch who had betrayed him. His crew could scarcely keep him from killing her on the spot.

In the twenty-five years between John's death and her own, Susannah Kent liked to predict that, after she was gone, no one would thrive on Kent Island. For a long time it seemed that the

The buildings originally used by Sterling Rockefeller's bird sanctuary were renovated to be used as the Warden's house, left, and the dormitory at the Scientific Station on Kent Island. (BC)

Students at Bowdoin College keeping in touch with the outside world via short-wave radio, 1935. (BC)

prophecy might hold true, because no one who attempted to settle there ever stayed and prospered, and the island remained more or less unoccupied for many years. In 1920, McLaughlin Brothers bought the property. They pastured sheep there, took young cattle there to fatten during the summers, and operated a herring weir. The resident caretaker made part of his lonely living by gardening and fishing. Twice a year, his solitude was interrupted. In the spring, visitors came to pick gulls' eggs, and Passamaquoddy Indians came from Pleasant Point, Maine, for their annual hunting, fishing and gathering pilgrimage. In the fall, duck hunters broke the silence. In both seasons, lobster fishermen camped on the little islands while they tended their traps. It was the caretaker's house, barn and sheds that Allan Moses and Ralph Griffin used when they operated Sterling Rockefeller's bird sanctuary, and it was these buildings that Bowdoin College renovated to use as dormitories, offices and laboratories.

Bill Gross became the first field director of the Bowdoin College Scientific Station, and his advisory committee consisted mainly of powerful Bowdoin alumni such as Commander Donald B. Macmillan, Sterling Rockefeller, and Professor Alfred O. Gross. Albert T. Gould and Sumner T. Pike, a wealthy Lubec, Maine, businessman, ran the financial campaign. Bill Gross soon accumulated food, gasoline and library books, and the College was loaned one of the best medium-powered short-wave radio transmitters then available. Gross acquired two boats: the *Zacatecas*, designed and built for the Scientific Station and donated by Alger W. Pike of Lubec, and the older *Bowdoin II*, which had been part of the Rockefeller gift.

The party that set off from the Pike sardine plant in Lubec to spend the summer of 1935 on Kent Island included ten students, a commissary officer, a cook, a radio operator and a boatman. Two forty-foot boats were loaded deep for the passage to Kent Island, a trip of some twenty-five miles across the Grand Manan Channel and around the northern end of Grand Manan. The "expedition" cleared customs at North Head and then continued to their isolated destination six miles east of Grand Manan's southern tip.

Ernest Joy welcomed the newcomers, and they began to settle themselves in their summer home. They set up generating plants and a telephone intercom system; they transferred the precious donated books from their packing cases to the library shelves; and they installed their short-wave transmitter. On a daily schedule, they began to communicate with the Army Signal Corps in Baltimore and another station in West Acton, Massachusetts. At that time, radio had been in popular use for little more than a decade and was still something of a novelty, but the Bowdoin radio was sophisticated enough that messages could be sent both by voice and by telegraph code. In addition to their regular contacts in New England, the operators enjoyed exchanges with ham radio operators as far away as Hungary and Russia. A portable transmitter was even installed aboard *Bowdoin II*, probably the earliest marine radio in the Grand Manan area.

With accommodations and equipment in place, the students began their ornithology projects. An immense colony of herring gulls monopolized the southern section of Kent Island. After the Migratory Birds Act came into effect, the herring gull population had exploded, and now the Scientific Station would participate in an international survey, sponsored by the governments of Canada and the United States, to learn more about the species. Kent Island became the lead station in a chain of herring gull banding sites along the Atlantic seaboard. The great black-backed gull had moved from its traditional range much farther north to nest along the more southerly Atlantic coast, extending its range south of Connecticut. Why had the habits of this, the largest species of gull common in this part of the world, changed so much? Black guillemots, Leach's storm-petrels, razorbills, Atlantic puffins, and arctic and common terns also served as study subjects. The students banded thousands of young birds, including the upland species found on Kent and other islands, and they contributed their findings to the cumulative life-histories of the birds they studied.

Early in the life of the Scientific Station, Bowdoin decided to open the Kent Island facilities to any qualified graduates and undergraduates of other colleges and universities for whom they had dormitory space. They made a point of not discriminating against applicants on the basis of "race, creed, colour, or national origin" and, after about 1953, they did not discriminate on the basis of sex, either.

In the summer of 1937, Albert A. Brand, a research associate at Cornell University, conducted one of the earliest experiments in a new branch of study, the first of its kind to be carried out anywhere. He transmitted the calls and songs of birds by radio for recording on disks and on film sound tracks. Unable to get the heavy sound recording truck to Kent Island, Brand's team left the unit on the mainland at Ingalls Head, five miles away. Then they picked up bird songs with sensitive microphones, fed them by cable to the Station's radio shack, and broadcast them over their own short-wave transmitter to the sound truck at Ingalls Head.

This method worked extremely well, except for recording the songs of Leach's storm-petrels, which like to sing in subdued tones on foggy nights. A parabolic reflector that picked up faint sounds from up to a mile away soon solved that problem. The transmission and recording of this "natural music" drew headlines in the Boston papers in the summer and fall of 1937, and the accomplishment remained unique for over two decades. "Until 1961," reported Cornell's Laboratory of Ornithology, "the only records we have had of Leach's storm-petrels were from Kent Island and the studies made of the herring gull made in the Kent Island colony are still our best recordings. Both of these recordings were included in the *Field Guide to Bird Songs* which matches Roger Tory Peterson's *Field Guide*."

One of the questions tackled repeatedly by researchers at Kent Island has been, how do migratory birds navigate? During the summer of 1938, Don Griffin conducted the first experiments in the continuing study of the homing powers of the Leach's storm-petrel, one of the bird kingdom's most interesting navigators.

Leach's storm-petrels are strictly pelagic, living on and travelling over the ocean and putting ashore only to nest. Scientists have given Leach's storm-petrels a long official name, *Oceanodroma leucorhoa leucorhoa,* and they have been working at providing a biography to match. These mysterious birds average eight inches in length, and in colour they are sooty brown with contrasting white upper tail coverts. The tail is forked, and the wings are long and pointed. Perhaps 2,200 of the Grand Manan archipelago's pairs nest on Kent Island. Having spent months wandering over the Atlantic, the males arrive in late spring and begin to prepare nests. Not satisfied with surface homes, they burrow into the earth, often as far as three feet, before setting up a simple nest for their mates. Second year and older males go directly to their own burrows, while younger males must begin a massive excavating task comparable to a human's shifting tons of soil and rock with earth-moving equipment. Then, in the dark of the night during the stillness of early June, the males come out of their burrows and begin their sonar-like mating calls. Females, soaring high overhead, answer in kind, until each has been guided down to earth to her mate's burrow. This drama is played out not only in darkness, but usually in fog as well.

Don Griffin began to try to unravel the petrels' migratory mysteries. At night, he gathered up to eighty birds, put them in crates, and exposed them to various methods of disorientation. Then groups of birds were taken by the Station's boat or Grand Manan fishing craft to connect with the wider-ranging ships that would release them. Canadian National freighters carried one group of birds out of Halifax and set them free near the middle of the Gulf Stream, and another group of birds were sent on their way from the Yarmouth to Boston ferry in the Gulf of Maine. Robert Parker, Grand Manan district superintendent of government telegraphs, coordinated these elaborate shipping plans by radio and telegraph. Before long, Griffin could record, most of the petrels returned, at night and often in foggy weather. This success inspired Griffin to became a pilot so he could fly in pursuit of homing gulls and, later, he became widely known for his knowledge of bats and their ability to navigate by

Installing meteorological component of the "outdoor laboratory"
on Kent Island, 1936. (BC)

sound. Three years later, James Blunt, a Bowdoin pre-medical graduate and the 1940 field director, carried out research to find out whether gulls' migrating instinct was connected with their thyroid glands.

The Scientific Station experimenters were not all ornithologists. By 1936, Bill Gross was a graduate student at the Harvard Geography School, under Dr. Charles Brooks, director of Harvard's Blue Hill Observatory. Brooks had helped create the observatory on Mount Washington, New Hampshire, and was a founder of the American Meteorological Society. Gross persuaded Brooks to establish yet another weather station, and soon two young meteorologists took all the necessary equipment to Kent Island. By radio and by mail, they began to feed weather data from that region into the North American reports and records. Among the researchers attracted to the Bowdoin "outdoor laboratory" by this weather station was Fred Sargent, who had been fascinated by the effects of weather on human health since adolescence. During the summers of 1939 and 1941, he based a project on an unusual weather pattern characteristic of Kent Island. There, in the summer, when a cold front passes and the barometric pressure rises, the temperature goes up instead of down. Comparing experiments carried out on the island with identical studies done in a place with an ordinary weather pattern would, Sargent thought, shed light on the causes of the common cold. Later, Sargent became president of the International Society of Biometeorology and director of the Centre of Human Ecology at the University of Illinois.

Robert M. (Bob) Cunningham, now known throughout the world for his work in meteorology, first arrived at the Station in June 1937, as a high school student from the Cambridge School in Weston, Massachusetts, to keep the weather records. When he returned in 1938, his assignments expanded to include helping Lester Tate build a new radio shack and milking Alice the cow. In 1939, he returned for another stint as a student. Out of those early years came his first published article, "Chloride Content of Fog Water in Relation to Air Trajectory" — one of the oldest chemical analyses of fog water. Because he did his study out in the Bay of Fundy, miles from industrial sites, it remains a benchmark in the investigation into that modern plague, acid rain. Over forty years later, after a distinguished career in meteorology, Bob found himself back at Kent Island in the summers of 1983 and 1984, with fellow researchers Peter Summers and Hari Samant, collecting fog samples for an acid rain study for the Canadian Atmospheric Environment Service.

Even though Bob Cunningham's career led him to many parts of the world, he continued to take responsibility for the Kent Island weather observations and records. Several times a year, Ernest Joy would send his readings to Bob wherever he might be, always accompanied by a letter written in the caretaker's unique style. (Seventy of his letters are on file in the archives of the Grand Manan museum.) After one long silence due to Bob's involvement with defense work, Ernest ended his message with, "For heaven's sake, write and tell me if you are alive or dead!"

Ernest's concern was real; the war had began to affect Grand Manan. On October 1, 1939, just weeks after Canada declared war on Germany, he received orders to keep off the air. He had hoped to make at least one daily radio contact with the Life Saving Station at Outer Wood Island, but even that was forbidden. Ernest (by then a widower) and his housekeeper Carrie Chase were completely cut off from the outside world. For the next two summers, students broke

Bob Cunningham, left, and Peter Summers of the Atmospheric Environment Service, Toronto, standing by the fog screen collector at Kent Island, 1984. (R.M. Cunningham)

their solitude, but Japan's attack on Pearl Harbour closed down the Station's research programme for three years. Early in 1940, Ernest reported having seen no U-boats in the Bay of Fundy, but two years later he revealed, "There have been a lot of things floating around . . . lumber, lard, coffee, airplane parts and dead men . . . four bodies have been found around Grand Manan. Lee Wilcox picked one up off South West Head, and one at Gannet Rock, and one went ashore at Long Island. I picked up some lumber and one bucket of lard — I got the pail and the gulls got the lard."

Although Bob Cunningham instructed Air Force students in meteorology at M.I.T. and did research on aircraft icing from a winter base in Minnesota, the only time he experienced the "shooting war" was on Kent Island. In the spring of 1942, he and Myhron Tate (Lester Tate's son) visited Ernest Joy at the Station, combining weather business with a social call. On the boat trip over from Ingalls Head, Bob and Myhron had noticed aircraft headed out into the Bay of Fundy, but thought little of it. Ever since the Commonwealth Air Training Station had been established at Pennfield, on the New Brunswick mainland, planes were a common sight, easily recognized as "friendlies." Though the manoeuvres sometimes annoyed the fishermen, they accepted them as just another wartime nuisance. Suddenly, near the end of Bob and Myhron's visit at the Station, a low-flying plane heading back to home base began strafing the island. Bob later said, "the shooting was impressive for a while, before we realized we were too close to the action." All the shots missed, and Bob charitably suggests that "gulls on a presumably deserted island" had been the targets of the trigger-happy airmen. A less kindly view might be that, if they were training observers on that flight, they might have seen a group of people in the open field gaping at them in shock and disbelief.

When the war ended, life at the Scientific Station resumed. Dr. K.C.M. Sills, Bowdoin's president, visited this "unique possession" in 1948. In his report to the board of governors, he not only praised the work of Ernest Joy, "certainly a very fine servant of the College," but also successfully appealed for more realistic funding. That year, the Station's total budget had been $850, and of that, Ernest's salary accounted for $360. The increase came too late for Ernest, however. Carrie Chase died of a heart attack on September 10, 1948. The solitude of the following winter, added to the after-effects of influenza, dulled Ernest's normal zest for living. Finally, determined not to spend another winter at the Station, he resigned his position and left Kent Island for the last time in early November, 1949. Two years later, at the age of 74, he, too, suffered a heart attack and died. His death grieved the Kent Island alumni, scattered across the United States and beyond. They revered this man of many talents, a naturalist, entertainer and teacher who had alerted them to many things never found in textbooks.

It was some time before Bowdoin College could find a permanent replacement for Ernest Joy. For awhile, no one lived on the island in the winter but, without year-round security, the Station's buildings and equipment soon became targets of vandals. After the College decided to hire a permanent caretaker again, several Grand Manan men rotated on the job. Finally, in 1963, Myhron Tate took it over, and he kept it

Myhron Tate, caretaker of the Bowdoin College Scientific Station, 1963-1982. (M. and E. Tate)

for nearly two decades. His efficient services have been acknowledged in several scientific reports and, like Ernest Joy before him, he has become a lifelong friend to many students. Myhron was succeeded by his son, Robert, who held the position of caretaker for several years.

Professor Alfred Gross retired in 1953 after eighteen years as director of the Scientific Station, and he was succeeded by Dr. Charles E. Huntington. In the post-war economic boom, there was a great surge in all kinds of scientific investigation. Wartime technologies were adapted for peacetime uses, including the study of nature. Huntington applied new technology to his studies of Leach's storm-petrel, and he also fostered an interest in the investigation among the island's summer students.

It was once thought that the breeding colonies in the Grand Manan archipelago were the largest on the Atlantic coast. Through banding and other observations, Huntington became convinced that there was another heavily populated nesting area somewhere in the region. When he found it in Newfoundland/Labrador, the discovery surprised ornithologists, few of whom had known about this massive concentration of "fork-tails." But Leach's storm-petrels, says Dr. Huntington, "are navigators whose secrets are mostly still hidden," and he contin-

Charles Huntington and family, Kent Island, 1965. (M. and E. Tate)

ued the effort to unravel these mysteries. As a test of the birds' unerring instincts, he devised a more ambitious version of Don Griffin's early experiment. Specially banded petrels were taken to Great Britain aboard an Air Canada flight and released after dark. As expected, they returned by night to their own burrows on Kent Island, one of them after a mere nine-day flight from Scotland.

Later Kent Island experiments have shown that petrels use a sense of smell, not present in most birds, to help them zero in on their own burrows. Researchers at the Station have also found that petrels prefer to live most of their breeding life, in or out of the nest, in darkness, because their enemies, the great black-backed gulls, keep active on clear nights as well as during the day. Hence, fog is a blessing to them.

Fascinating as they are to ornithologists, Leach's storm-petrels have not pushed common eiders into second-class citizenship on Kent Island. On the contrary, all who study at the Station take an interest in the eiders' welfare, regardless of their own special investigations. Throughout the years, researchers made many discoveries about the common eider's life and habits. In 1974 and 1975, telemetry helped Edward O. Minot, a grandson of Dr. Alfred O. Gross, in his study of the eiders' breeding ecology. The Canadian Wildlife Service had used telemetry to study the movements of large land mammals such as polar bears and caribou, and now Minot tried it with birds. Nine nesting females, properly tagged and banded for visual observation, were fitted with tiny transmitters and released, after sighting and reception points had been established and manned. The broadcast range was about six miles from a bird on the

water, so the feathered radio operators could be followed, first
to Wood Island off Seal Cove, and thence out Seal Cove Sound
as far as South West Head on the tip of the main island.

While telemetry aided Minot's investigations, his experiments
and those of others proved the limits of the technology at that
time. Although the tiny radio unit weighed less than an ounce,
it was still too heavy and bulky even for a bird the size of an
eider. But Minot's thesis gave ample proof that Allan Moses's vi-
sion for Kent Island had become a reality. In the third year after
the sanctuary was established under Allan's supervision, there
were 178 occupied eider nests. In 1937, the third year of the
Scientific Station's operation, there were 300 nests containing
eggs. When Minot carried out his study in 1974-75, he found
that:

> Eiders nest on all islands of the Grand Manan Ar-
> chipelago. The total adult and sub-adult female
> population, based on 1975 counts, is ca. 7,000.
> Nest surveys made in 1974 indicated that ca.
> 3,500 females nested, although this figure may be
> low.

The eiders, once so scarce, had taken up all the suitable nesting space on Kent and Hay Islands and overflowed to most of
the secure locations on other islands.

In 1986, Charles Huntington retired as head of the Bowdoin
biology department, but he stayed on as director of the Scientific Station until 1988 to establish continuity with his successor,
Dr. Nathaniel T. Wheelwright. Dr. Wheelwright set about his
new responsibilities with vigour and enthusiasm. First, he obtained $47,000 in grants to purchase new equipment:
microcomputers, computerized field data loggers, sophisticated
meteorological equipment, and a photovoltaic system to generate the Station's electricity. The Grand Manan archipelago is one
of the foggiest areas of the region, and Kent Island is in the foggiest part of the archipelago. In 1967, 63 of the 92 observation
days showed fog, and the summer of 1989 was not far behind

that record. Still, Wheelwright's system collected enough solar energy to provide "quiet, renewable electricity for the station" on all but three or four days.

Even though he has made sure that Kent Island has the most modern equipment, Wheelwright says, "The wonderful simple atmosphere of the station should change little." Under his supervision, the Scientific Station continues to carry on the work started by Allan Moses. Its success, built on the efforts, first of Allan Moses and then of Sterling Rockefeller, Ernest Joy, Alfred O. and Bill Gross, Lester and Myhron Tate, Bob Cunningham, Chuck Huntington, Nathaniel Wheelwright, and many others, has proved the widow Kent to be a false prophet.

The Grand Manan Museum and Nature Centre

In 1950, Grade Twelve was added to the New Brunswick school system, automatically increasing the school-age population; the baby-boom generation was making its inevitable progress through the system; and a successful programme lowered the drop-out rate. By the 1960s, the high school that had opened in 1948 couldn't possibly accommodate the burgeoning student population. As home rooms began moving into the basement of the school, the Moses Museum's future appeared to be at stake.

The board of school trustees faced a dilemma. Packing up and storing away the natural history collection, even temporarily and with the best of intentions, would break the trust agreement that it be kept on display in perpetuity, and this unpalatable action would release only one classroom. Another solution would have been to house junior classes in the high school building and force older students to finish their high school studies on the mainland. But complete on-island high school education had been the selling point when the original parish districts were persuaded to consolidate two decades earlier, and such a retrogressive step could not be contemplated.

Island rate-payers had to consider two urgent needs. The

high school had to have even more space than would be created by moving out the Moses collection, and the collection must have its own specially designed building. Indeed, local history enthusiasts had hoped for a separate museum building long before Allan Moses had deeded his collection to the community.

Despite objections to an increased tax burden, the rate-payers overwhelmingly approved the capital expenditure to construct additional high school facilities. Laboratory and shop space had been particularly cramped, and to correct that situation, the board opted for a separate building for the instruction of senior students.

Grand Manan chose a good time in the political history of New Brunswick for its new project. Because the government of Premier Louis J. Robichaud had just introduced its new "Equal Opportunity" policy, the grants to the island community were more generous than they would have been earlier. As another consequence of its isolation, the island's school system escaped the consolidation with other regional districts mandated by the new programme. Grand Manan remained a district unto itself, the smallest of thirty-three districts in the new provincial system. The new Grand Manan High School was opened for use in 1967, under the direction of J. Peter Kilburn, then supervising principal.

While the board of school trustees concentrated on filling the need for better high school facilities, the faculty spearheaded the drive for a museum building. Fortunately, several members of the board were also interested in heritage preservation and strongly supported the plan, and soon other interested citizens became involved in the campaign. Realizing they could not look to the school district for financial support, the museum group appealed in March 1961, to Robert Tweedie, director of the New Brunswick Travel Bureau, who was aware of the museum's value in attracting summer visitors to Grand Manan. Within a few months, this appeal elicited a grant of $10,000, which the committee locked away to accumulate interest.

Letters patent issued on June 5, 1962, incorporated a body named Gerrish House Society for the purpose of building and operating a museum and science centre, with collections in human and natural history, including documents and works of art, and for carrying out related programmes. The museum was not to be simply a repository; its operators were "to encourage the education of children and adults in the natural sciences and in local history." As a non-profit corporation, the Society became a charitable organization for income tax purposes.

A special advisory committee included enthusiastic mainland supporters of the movement representing several fields of interest. Dr. Frank Toole, Vice-President of the University of New Brunswick, chaired the committee, thus linking it to the University. Milton F. Gregg, VC, former president of U.N.B. and, like Dr. Toole, a summer resident of Grand Manan, joined the group of distinguished advisors. Dr. Charles Huntington provided a link with the Kent Island programme. Individually and collectively, these special advisors helped to open many doors that otherwise might have remained closed.

The museum organizers chose the Society's name to honour Moses Gerrish, one of the Loyalist leaders at the time of the community's permanent settlement in 1784. The Society would serve as an interim umbrella for related activities. One such objective was achieved shortly following incorporation.

The Grand Manan Historical Society had been organized and incorporated in 1931, largely through the efforts of summer resident Buchanan Charles, of Brookline, Massachusetts. On May 6, 1934, the Historical Society organized an observance of the 150th anniversary of the founding of the community which included an exhibition of artifacts and photography. At the beginning of World War II, the Society became inactive, but not before Charles had published six issues of *The Grand Manan Historian* and a definitive map of Grand Manan. In 1962, when Charles knew that an Island museum would be established, he agreed to repatriate the documents and archives he had gathered. In the following year, a new editor published Volume VII of the *Historian*, and the series was continued. Leon G. Small became the new president of the Historical Society and held the position for sixteen years.

In 1963, the first summer exhibition of the new museum was set up temporarily in the former I.L. Newton store in Grand Harbour, and the store building also served as a base for the first Summer School of Nature, headed by Wayne Guptill. This programme attracted well over a hundred young students, and it has carried on successfully each year since then. Weather permitting, classes are held outdoors in any one of a score of natural laboratory sites.

When building a new museum became the Island's major capital project to commemorate Canada's Centennial, the project attracted even more community support. To celebrate the Centennial, the federal government offered capital grants to assist with heritage projects, and Grand Manan's application for a grant to build the museum was approved. A renewed fundraising campaign supplemented the grant with donations from the public and from other private sources. With sufficient funds, the Gerrish House Society was ready to build. They acquired an ideal site across the highway from the high school, and a local construction firm, McDowell & Cook, agreed to put up the building at cost. Local truckers organized hauling bees, and landed a generous supply of grading as their contribution.

An overflow crowd poured into the Grand Manan Museum and Nature Centre for the official opening on July 23, 1967. The Moses Memorial Collection, properly arranged and cased by David S. Christie, then a naturalist at Fundy National Park, occupied over half of the main floor. Recorded bird songs, a gift of Cornell University's Department of Ornithology, filled that area with natural music that included interludes from the early Kent Island experiments. Domestic artifacts and collections that Eric Allaby had brought up from historic shipwrecks in the archipelago were displayed, and a combined office, library and archives already held valuable collections. A picture window, the only opening in the rear wall, gave a panoramic view of Ross Island, the site of the first European settlement on Grand Manan, as well as the lovely harbour and the great Bay of Fundy. Downstairs an area had been set aside for a display, later designed and installed by the Univeristy of New Brunswick Department of

The Moses Memorial
Collection, case #1.

(Eric Allaby)

The Grand Manan Museum.   (Eric Allaby)

Geology, that would tell the intriguing story of the geology of Grand Manan, "an open textbook on the subject." Downstairs, too, was the artifact storage room and the large Nature Centre, with its own library and classroom for use in stormy weather. On the front lawn, a new Canadian maple leaf flag snapped in the afternoon breeze from a strong, straight flagpole of Douglas fir. Capt. Leonard Guptill, Jr. had brought this centennial gift from British Columbia aboard his new vessel, built on the West Coast. In the back yard, visitors could inspect the one-room Deep Cove School, donated to the museum by Mrs. Victor LaFoley. Just as the sun set, the drum corps of the First Battalion, "Green Howards" Regiment, Yorkshire, England, beat the "Retreat" to a memorable day.

The collections of the Grand Manan Museum and Nature Centre have continued to grow through gifts of artifacts and archival material. These collections provide research data for an active Genealogical Society. The Walter B. McLaughlin Marine Gallery was added in 1979, with the help of a grant from the National Museums of Canada and local funds. Its focal point is the beautiful crystal lens from Gannet Rock lighthouse, donated by the federal Department of Transport after it installed modern automatic equipment on the Rock.

Of the many people who have given devoted service to the museum, one in particular deserves special mention. Charles Titus became the volunteer custodian as soon as the building was completed. In addition to his other duties, he hoisted the flag in the morning and lowered it at sundown for as long as he was able to walk the distance from his home. His death was a great loss to the community and to the museum. Almost all of the museum work was, and is, done by volunteers. Audrey Ingalls sat in the president's chair for many years, Elmer Wilcox put in lengthy service as secretary, and Marilyn Cary managed the Summer School of Nature, handling registration and recruiting instructors. Today, Otis Green is president of Grand Manan Museum Inc. (the corporate successor of the Gerrish House Society), and Audrey Ingalls is secretary-treasurer. From 1969 until 1987, Eric Allaby, an author, artist, and underwater archaeologist, served as curator. Now, Wendy Dathan is curator and Glen-eta Hettrick oversees the extensive archives.

To many, the museum has become the "long house" of local human history and tradition, enhanced as in real life by displays of the natural world. But, central as it is to community life, it has more than local appeal. Many of the thousands who have visited Grand Manan in the summers since 1967 are avid bird watchers or professional naturalists. They come to the museum now as former generations used to visit the Moses home a century ago, when this story had its real beginning. The museum perpetuates this tradition and links the Island's human and natural history to that of a greater world environment. Had it not been for the urgent need to provide suitable accommodation for the Moses Memorial Collection, no museum would have opened in 1967. Without the drive for a museum sparked by the collection, the archives would doubtless have become impossible to repatriate, and the archival collection could not have gained the stature and value, local and international, that it holds today.

In the same vein, Bowdoin College would probably have found itself an off-campus nature laboratory without Allan Moses, but it would not have been located at Kent Island, nor would it have begun operation as early as in 1935. While support and catalysts were ready in each case, both the Grand Manan Museum and Nature Centre and the Bowdoin College Scientific Station on Kent Island owe their lives to the contributions of one man, Allan Moses.

As well as offering a glimpse into a unique life, the likes of which will never be seen again, this record will show how it all came about.

Bibliography

Bibliography of Related Works

Anon. "Petrels' Songs Captured and Sent by Radio: Bowdoin's Expedition to Kent Island Accomplishes Feat For First Time," *Boston Transcript* (August 2, 1937).

Anon. "Bird Songs and Calls Are Recorded by Scientists From Bowdoin College," *Boston Herald* (November 18, 1937).

Baird, S.F. "Notes on Certain Aboriginal Shell Mounds on the Coast of New Brunswick and of New England," Miscellaneous Collections 22 (1882) Smithsonian Institution, Washington, D.C. (See also Proceedings of the United States Museum.)

Chapin, J.P. *Birds of the Belgian Congo*, Bulletin, American Museum of Natural History 65 (1932).

Cilley, Jonathan Prince. *Bowdoin Boys in Labrador — 1906.* Rockland, Maine.

Dixon, Chester A. [Island Courier section] *St. Croix Courier* (12 December 1929).

Estabrooks, Barry. "What Price Wildlife," *Equinox* 4:20 (March-April 1985), 83.

Fewkes, J. Walter. "A Zoological Reconnaissance in Grand

Manan," *American Naturalist* 24 (1890), 423-428, rpt. *Grand Manan Historian* 20.

Godfrey, W. Earl. "A Tribute to Robie Tufts, 1884-1982," *Canadian Field Naturalist* 98, 513-518.

Griffin, Donald R. "Homing Experiments With Leach's Petrels on Kent Island," *Fourth Annual Report of the Bowdoin Scientific Station* (April 1939), 24-25.

Ingersoll, L.K. "Winged Earthlings Range Sea, Puzzle Scientists," *Saint Croix Courier* (April 14, 1960), 9, 12.

_____ . "Simeon Frankland Cheney, an Early New Brunswick Naturalist," *The Sands of Time*, Grand Manan Genealogical Society, 1 (September, 1980). Rev. version *N.B. Naturalist/Le Naturaliste du N-B* 14 (1985), 143-146.

Land Transfer Records, Charlotte County Registry Office, St. Andrews, N.B.

Lewis, Harrison. "History of the Canadian Wildlife Service" MS. Public Archives of Canada PAC RG 109, vol. 1.

Lorimer, J.G. *History of the Islands and Islets of the Bay of Fundy.* St. Stephen, N.B.: *St. Croix Courier*, 1876.

McDonald, Donald (Deputy Surveyor) "A General Report on the General List of Applications for Land in the County of Charlotte," 1 January, 1806. MS, Crown Lands Office, Fredericton, N.B.

Mitchell, Elsie. "Bill Gunn: An Ear for Nature," *Nature Canada* (January-March, 1985), 9-10.

Moses, Allan L. African journal series, ed. Sarah E. M. Smith,

Saint Croix Courier (February 7, March 7, April 11, August 1, 1929; January 23, 1930).

Murphy, Robert Cushman. "Notes on Tubinares, Including Records Which Affect the AOU Check-list," *The Auk* 39 (1922), 58.

Murray, Bee. "Kent Island, a Rugged Outpost of Science," *Boston Herald* (September 22, 1940).

Rockefeller, J. Sterling, and Charles G.B. Murphy. "The Rediscovery of Pseudocalyptomena," *The Auk* 50 (1932), 23-29.

Rockwell, Robert H. "Under Sail to the Cape Verdes; The Voyage of the 'Blossom,' on a Deep-Sea Cruise for Oceanic Birds," *Natural History* 31 (1931), 651-652.

_____ . "Sailing to Senegambia," *Natural History* 31 (1932), 167-180.

_____ . "Southward Through the Doldrums," *Natural History* 32 (1932), 424-436.

Sargent, Frederick, and Thomas Ippolito, M.D. "Phases of Physiological Response to Meteorological Stimuli." *Fifth Annual Report of the Bowdoin Scientific Station* (February 1, 1941), 33-35.

Sclanders, Ian. "This New Brunswick: A Parade of People and Places," Saint John *Telegraph-Journal* (November 13, 1937).

Simmons, George Finlay. "Sinbads of Science: Narrative of the Voyage of the Windjammer 'Blossom' to the Sargasso Sea and Senegambian Africa, and Among the Islands of High Adventure in the South Atlantic," *National Geographic Magazine* 52 (1927), 1-75.

Smith, Sarah E[lizabeth] M[oses]. "The Migratory Birds Convention Act and Some Stories of the Labrador Patrol." MS, Archives, Grand Manan Museum.

Squires, W. Austin Squires. *The Birds of New Brunswick* 2nd ed. Saint John: New Brunswick Museum, 1976.

Publications Related to the
Bowdoin College Scientific Station

This is a partial list. Complete, up-to-date lists can be found in the annual reports of the Bowdoin College Scientific Station.

A. Journal Articles

1935 - 1939

Gross, Alfred O. "Birds of the Bowdoin-Macmillan Arctic Expedition," Auk 54 (1939), 12-42.

_____ . "Eider Ducks of Kent Island," *The Auk* 55 (1938), 387-400.

Gross, Thomas A.O. "Designing the First Stage of the Speech Amplifier," QST 21:12 (1937), 33-100; Radio Station VE1 IN

_____ . "Operation of the Zero-Bias Modulators," *Radio* 230 (1938), 387 - 400.

Gross, William A.O. "The Life History Cycle of Leach's Petrel (*Oceanodroma leucorhoa leucorhoa*) on the Outer Sea Islands of the Bay of Fundy," *The Auk* 52 (1935), 382-399.

_____ . "Kent's Island — Outpost of Science," *Natural History Magazine* 37 (March 1936), 195-210.

Pettingill, Olin S., Jr. "The Bird Life of the Grand Manan Archipelago," *Proceedings of the Nova Scotian Institute of Science* 19: part IV (1939), 293-372.

1940-1949

Cunningham, Robert M. "Chloride Content of Fog Water in Relation to Air Trajectory," *Bulletin of American Meteorological Society* 22 (1941), 17-20. (Reprinted as #8 in the Contribution Series.)

Griffin, Donald R. "Homing Experiments with Leach's Storm Petrels," *The Auk* 57 (1940), 61-74.

Gross, Alfred O. "The Migration of Kent Island Herring Gulls," *Bird-banding* 11 (1940), 129-155.

_____ . "Food of the Snowy Owl," *The Auk* 611 (1944), 1-18.

_____ . "The Present Status of the American Eider on the Maine Coast," *Wilson Bulletin* 56 (1944), 15-26.

_____ . "The Present Status of the Double-crested Cormorant on the Coast of Maine," *The Auk* 61 (1944), 513-537.

_____ . "The Present Status of the Great Black-backed Gull on the Coast of Maine," *The Auk* 62 (1945), 241-256.

_____ . "The Laughing Gull of the Coast of Maine," *Bird-banding* 16 (1945), 53-54.

_____ . "The Black Duck Nesting on the Outer Coastal Islands of Maine," *The Auk* 62 (1945), 620-622.

_____ . "Recoveries of Banded Leach's Storm Petrels," Bird-banding 18 (1947), 117-126.

_____ . "Cyclic Invasions of the Snowy Owl and the Migration of 1945-1946," *The Auk* 64 (1947), 584-601.

_____ . "Gulls of Muskeget Island," *Bulletin of Massachusetts Audubon* Society 32 (1948), 43-47.

Paynter, Raymond A., Jr. "The Fate of Banded Kent Island Herring Gulls," *Bird-banding* 18 (1947), 156-170.

_____ . "Clutch-size and the Egg and Chick Mortality of Kent Island Herring Gulls," *Ecology* 30 (1949), 146-166.

Poor, Hustace M. "Colour-banded Adult Herring Gulls," *Bird-banding* 15 (1944), 112-114.

Winn, Howard E. "The Black Guillemots of Kent Island," *Bulletin of Massachusetts Audubon Society* 31 (1947), 160-162.

1950-1959

Huntington, Charles E. "Age Discrimination in a Breeding Colony of the Herring Gull, *Larus argentatus*," Acta XI Congress of International Ornithologists (1955), 467-469.

Paynter, Raymmond A., Jr. "Clutch-size and Egg Mortality of Kent Island Eiders," *Ecology* 32 (1951), 497-507.

_____ . "Interrelations Between Clutch-size, Brood-size, Pre-fledgling Survival and Weight in Kent Island Tree Swallows," *Bird-banding* 25 (1954), 35-38, 102-110, 136-148.

Winn, Howard E. "The Black Guillemots of Kent Island," *The Auk* 67 (1950), 477-485.

1960-1969

Benton, Allen H.. and Vaughnda Shatreu. "Notes on a Collection of Bird Fleas From Grand Manan, New Brunswick," *Canadian Entomologist* 94 (1962), 743-745.

Billings, Susan M. "Homing in Leach's Petrel," *The Auk* 85 (1968), 36-43.

Bullock, Robert C. "The Intertidal Molluscan Fauna of Kent Island, New Brunswick, Canada," *Maine Field Naturalist* 17 (1961), 27-31.

Emlen, John T. Jr. "Determinants of Cliff Edge and Escape Responses in Herring Gull Chicks in Nature," *Behaviour* 22 (1963), 1-15.

Gobeil, Robert E. "Butterflies on Kent Island, New Brunswick," *Journal of Lepidopterists' Society* 19 (1965), 181-183.

_____ . "Unusual Records of Summer Birds on Kent Island, New Brunswick," *Canadian Field-Naturalist* 82 (1968), 203-209.

Hailman, Jack P. "The Ontogeny of an Instinct: The Pecking Response in Chicks of the Laughing Gull (*Larus atricilla L.*) and Related Species," *Behaviour* supp. 15 (1967), i-vii, 1-159.

Huntington, Charles E. "Population Dynamics of Leach's Storm Petrel, *Oceanodroma Leucorhoa*," Proceedings XIIIth International Ornithologists Congress (1963) 701-705.

Paynter, Raymond A., Jr. "A New Attempt to Construct Life Tables for Kent Island Herring Gulls," *Bulletin of Museum of Comparative Zoology* 133:11 (1966), 489-528.

1970-1979

Gill, Douglas E., William J.L. Sladen, and Charles E. Huntington. "A Technique for Capturing Petrels and Shearwaters at Sea," *Bird-banding* 41 (1970), 111-113.

Grubb, Thomas C. Jr. "Smell and Foraging in Shearwaters and Petrels," *Nature* 237 (1972), 404-405.

_____ . "Colony Location by Leach's Storm Petrels," *The Auk* 90 (1973), 78-82.

_____ . "Olfactory Navigation to the Nesting Burrow in Leach's Petrel (Oceanodroma leucorhoa)," *Animal Behaviour* 22 (1974), 192-202.

McCain, John. "A Vegetational Survey of Vascular Plants of the Kent Island Group, Grand Manan, New Brunswick," *Rhodora* 77 (1975), 196-209.

McCain, John W., R.B. Pike, and A.R. Hodgon, "The Vascular Flora of Kent Island, Grand Manan, New Brunswick," *Rhodora* 75 (1973), 311-322.

1980-1985

Huntington, Charles E. "Kent Island," *Maine Birdlife* 7:1 (Spring, 1985).

B. Theses (A Partial List)

The following theses are based to a considerable degree on work done at the Bowdoin Scientific Station:

Brisbin, I. Lehr, Jr. "A Quantitative Analysis of Ecological

Growth Efficiency in the Herring Gull." M.Sc., University of Georgia, 1965.

Dixon, Clara L. "A Population Study of Savannah Sparrows on Kent Island in the Bay of Fundy." Ph.D., University of Michigan, 1972.

Grubb, Thomas C., Jr. "Olfactory Navigation in Leach's Petrel and Other Procellariiform Birds." Ph.D., University of Wisconsin, 1971.

Hailman, Jack P. "The Ontogeny of an Instinct: The Pecking Response in Chicks of the Laughing Gull (Larus Atricilla L.) and Related Species." Ph.D., Duke University, 1964.

Minot, Edward O. "American Eider Rearing Ecology in the Grand Manan Archipelago, N.B." M.Sc., University of Maine, 1976.

Preston, William C. "Breeding Ecology and Social Behaviour of the Black Guillemot." Ph.D., University of Michigan, 1968.

Index